The Blessings of Bhutan

Russ and Blyth Carpenter

A Latitude 20 Book

UNIVERSITY OF HAWAI'I PRESS
HONOLULU

Printed in the United States of America

07 06   6 5 4 3 2

Library of Congress Cataloging-in-Publication Data
Carpenter, Russell B.
  The blessings of Bhutan / Russ and Blyth Carpenter.
    p. cm.
  Includes bibliographical references and index.
   ISBN-13: 978-0-8248-2679-6
   ISBN-10: 0-8248-2679-5 (pbk.: alk. paper)
  1. Bhutan. I. Carpenter, Blyth C. II. Title.
  DS491.4 .C37 2002
   954.98—dc21

                    2002031987

Keith Dowman has generously given permission to use extended quotations from *The Divine Madman*, translated by Keith Dowman, copyright 1980.

This book was produced in cooperation with the University of Hawai'i Press by Natural World Press, Inc.

CONTENTS

MAP OF BHUTAN

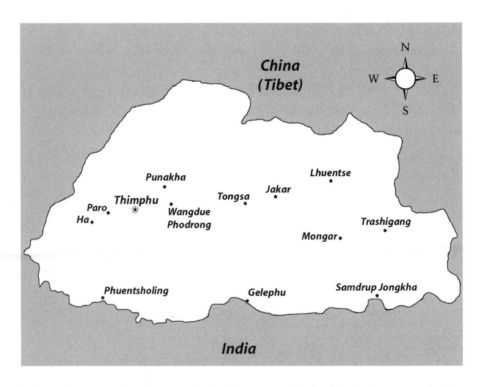

Note: spellings are based on *The Atlas of Bhutan,* published by the Ministry of Agriculture, Royal Government of Bhutan.

ACKNOWLEDGMENTS

This book could not have been written without the contributions of the following extraordinary people: Drew Carpenter, Pema Chhophyel, Karma Choden, Kesang Choden, Tashi Choki, Carol Crihfield, Kungzang Dechen, Nim Dem, Dasho Sherab Dorji, K.E.S Kirby Dorji, Kinley Dorji, Lopen Gyen Dorji, Singay Dorji, Thinley Dorji, Gaden Lam Jamyang, Janchu, Sonam Jatso, Tshewang Jigme, Dasho Shingkar Lam, Namgyel Lhendup, Lam Longyang, Karma Lotey, Dr. Paolo Morisco, Diana Myers, Rinzin Norbu, Karma C. Nyedrup, Namgey Om, Jigme Palden, Karma L. Rapten, Ugyen Rinzin, Tsewang Rixen, Khenpo Phuntsho Tashi, Sangay Tenzin, Sangey Tenzing, Karma C. Thinley, Kungzang Thinley, Kungzang Tobgay, Chado Tshering, Pelden Tshering, Gantey Tulku, Yangzom Ugyen, Karma Ura, Gregor Verhufen, Karma Wangchuck, Sangay Wangchuck, Thinley Wangchuck, Pema Wangda, Tshering Yangzom, Karma Yeshey, and Rinchen Yoezer.

Four people were especially generous: Sonam Jatso took us from one end of Bhutan to the other, patiently untangling the intricacies of Bhutanese culture. His friendship and intelligence have been remarkable. Karma Ura and K.E.S. Kirby Dorji have provided astute intellectual guidance, opening new vistas and saving us from some significant mistakes (all errors remaining in this book are attributable to us alone). Karma Lotey's steady, cheerful demeanor and affection remind us why Bhutan is a magic place.

All of the photographs in this book were taken by the authors except the photograph on the back cover, which was taken by Sherold Barr. The striking drawings in this book were done by Dasho Shingkar Lam, to whom we owe our heartfelt thanks. We express our esteem and appreciation to our friends at The University of Hawaii Press, including Bill Hamilton, Keith Leber, and Ann Ludeman.

Readers are welcome to contact the authors directly. Our email addresses are: russ@natworld.com and blyth@natworld.com.

Tashi Delek!

Introduction

This book explores one of the most improbable places on earth—Bhutan, the Dragon Kingdom. We will take you on a journey through sacred valleys in the last independent Buddhist state in the Himalayas. At the beginning, the place will seem exotic, and a long way from home. Later, your sense of the place will change. Bhutan will emerge as an extraordinary laboratory in which to examine questions of culture and values.

By the usual measurements, Bhutan appears inconsequential. It is a small, landlocked place in the Himalayas, with fewer than a million people. There are no traffic lights, no ATMs, and no McDonalds. Most roads are a lane and a half wide. The country has one airport, serving a handful of airplanes. There is one newspaper. Almost all Bhutanese people come from tiny villages, many of which are a two or three days' walk from the nearest roads.

But visitors often feel altered by Bhutan, sensing that they have traversed life-changing terrain. Their inner selves are stirred, even if they consider themselves seasoned and worldly-wise. They may be skeptical of pop-culture talk about "the wisdom of the East," and they may have their filters in place. Nevertheless, many come home with a nagging feeling that they were at the edge of learning something important, something primary.

That is what happened to us. When we went trekking in Bhutan in 1996, we thought we were well prepared, having been interested in Asia and Buddhism for 30 years. But after spending time in the Dragon Kingdom, we felt our anchors begin to drag. Somehow, this little country had perturbed a pair of focused, sequential Americans.

Not for the usual reasons, though. We did not become overnight Tantric Buddhists or students of a venerated lama. We did not feel captured by a Shangri-la. Instead, we felt the unseen forces of this place begin to take apart our intellectual and emotional houses. We became less sure of ourselves. Bhutan was giving us hints that it was time to take chances and to trust in a path that was invisible to us at the time, but might take us to worthwhile places.

At the end of that first trip, we knew we needed to return. But traveling to Bhutan has its complications. It is easy to go there as a tourist; it is more complicated wearing any other hat. We decided to become a two-person Peace Corps, trading our services for the chance to live among Bhutanese people. We had some luck. We uncovered an opportunity to go to work for a Bhutanese family that owned a little guest house, a construction company, and, most important for us, an old printing press. They wanted to upgrade to electronic publishing, and we had some skills as publishers.

We returned to Bhutan and helped establish the New Druk Sherig Press. Since then, we have returned many times. Our projects have diversified, ultimately including an Internet cafe, internet publishing for a scholarly journal, coaching for college admission exams, exporting Bhutanese textiles, learning Bhutanese archery, and establishing a radio communication system for remote villages. We have traveled from one end of the country to the other.

We never again went trekking in Bhutan. The mountains there are wonderful; the culture is even better. One of these days, we'll head for the high country again, but for the moment, the culture has us in its grip.

Our love for Bhutan is a sword with two edges. You probably have sensed the love by now; here are some hints about the other side. We observe cultural divides at every turn. We (the authors) are linear, the Bhutanese are intuitive. We are agnostic, the Bhutanese are Buddhist from birth. We watch the clock, the Bhutanese see time as a relatively unimportant element of life. We have a well-formed set of behaviors for business transactions; doing business in Bhutan can be, for us, an amorphous, puzzling experience. Sometimes differences like these are funny, but sometimes they are difficult and disturbing.

Where has this pathway taken us? Some of the measurements are easy. We have wonderful new friends, a renewed appreciation of art and folk crafts, and a much more thorough understanding of Himalayan religions. We can detect more flexibility and sensitivity in our lifestyle, which we know has come straight from Bhutan.

The most important thing about our experience is more subtle. Bhutanese culture has made us think. We feel a vitality in our thinking that is exhilarating and fundamental. We judge things now from many different perspectives, frequently landing on a point of view that is different from the one we would have held ten years ago. Slowly but surely, we seem to be improving our ability to focus on issues with quiet concentration. Among the many blessings of Bhutan, this training of the mind has been the deepest.

This book is organized in bite-size pieces we call "sketches." Think of them as essays whose job is to entertain and inform. Each sketch is meant to stand on its own feet. Thus it is not necessary to read them in order. Skip around, if that is your mood.

There is, however, a logical order to the sketches that you may find helpful. The book is divided into eight sections, each of which is introduced by a drawing of an important Bhutanese deity or symbol. This is how it works:

I.   Drawing of the Druk, the dragon symbol of Bhutan. An introduction to the culture and geography of Bhutan.

II.   Drawing of Drangsong, a local deity. A look at the ancient religion of Bhutan and how it connects to Buddhism and defines Bhutan's national sport of archery.

III.   Drawing of Guru Rinpoche, the 8th century Buddhist saint who brought Buddhism to the Himalayas and is now the most venerated figure in Bhutan. An introduction to some of the fascinating practices of Tantric Buddhism.

IV.   Drawing of Vajrapani, a wrathful meditational deity. Here, we examine Bhutanese art and medicine.

V.   Drawing of The Wheel of Law. Our thinking on the deep consequences of a belief in reincarnation, especially in the realm of environmental policy.

VI.   Drawing of the Dorje, the famous "thunderbolt" symbol of Himalayan Buddhism. We use the Dorje to introduce the subject of sexuality in Bhutanese culture and to become acquainted with Drukpa Kunley—one of the most appealing characters of all time.

VII.   Drawing of the female deity Tara. We examine the position of women in Bhutan.

VIII.   Drawing of the Lotus, one of the most familiar symbols of Buddhism throughout the world. We look at Bhutan's unique concept of "Gross National Happiness" and then ask what lies ahead for this remarkable country.

Before turning to the sketches, we will spend a moment on several fundamentals of religion in Bhutan. You will find certain Buddhist and pre-Buddhist ideas and words popping up constantly. That is inevitable, because Bhutan is framed by religious thinking (both old and new). While you will have plenty of time to explore this territory in the sketches, here are some basics you could fruitfully learn now.

Bhutan, Tibet, and other nearby regions are generally thought of as Buddhist cultures. This is correct, but seriously oversimplified. In fact, this part of the world had a vibrant religion in place before Buddhism arrived (sometime near the 8th century). The old religion is popularly referred to as "Bon"; Western scholars sometimes call it "The Religion with No Name." In any event, the old religion is still very important in Bhutan and fascinating in its own right. It does not get any press coverage in the West, but once you set foot in Bhutan, the old religion is pervasive.

When Buddhist missionaries arrived in the Himalayas, they faced the same question confronting missionaries everywhere; do we try to eradicate the indigenous beliefs, or do we accommodate them? In general, Buddhism has been quite willing to adapt to prevailing beliefs, and that is exactly what happened in Tibet, Bhutan, and surrounding areas. To this day, the blend of the old and new in Bhutan is breathtaking.

Buddhism in Bhutan is technically a branch of Tibetan Buddhism. We sometimes use that term in this book to include the Buddhism practiced in both Tibet and Bhutan. We more frequently use the term "Tantric Buddhism," which can be regarded as a synonym. (Yet another synonym is "Vajrayana," which is frequently heard in Bhutan, but is used rarely in the West.)

In Tibet, Buddhism has divided into four orders. Two of those became dominant in Bhutan: the Kagyu order, which is the state religion of Bhutan, and the Nyingma order. The Kagyus might be a little more structured and rule-oriented than the Nyingmas, but the differences are not major. By and large, the two orders in Bhutan get along respectfully. That was frequently not true in historical Bhutan and Tibet, when the various orders competed constantly and even killed each other on occasion.

The most important figure in Bhutanese culture is the 8th century larger-than-life character Guru Rinpoche. His image is everywhere (including the cover of this book). In fact, you might say that he is more important in Bhutan than the Buddha. According to the cosmology of Tantric Buddhism, there have been many Buddhas (one of whom was the "historical Buddha"). In contrast, there was only one Guru Rinpoche. Every place Guru Rinpoche visited in Bhutan is now a pilgrimage site, and his eight different manifestations are worshiped throughout the country. The Bhutanese tend to speak of Guru Rinpoche as if he were present at all times and in all places (and maybe he is). In one way or another, Guru Rinpoche has inspired a large part of the important teachings in Bhutan.

The legends of Guru Rinpoche have a tone you will encounter time and again in this book. Much of his life was spent subduing fierce local deities and evil spirits—both enemies of the Buddhist religion Guru Rinpoche was introducing to the Himalayas. Many other aspects of Bhutanese culture share this sense of confrontation and conquering, although the evil forces to be overcome may be disease, starvation, weather, and all the other forbidding aspects of carving out a life in the high country.

Finally, a few housekeeping items. Spelling is a problem in Bhutan. The Westernized spellings of Bhutanese languages are frequently inconsistent and nonphonetic. We have tried to present uniform spellings in this book, but if you find an inconsistencies, please forgive us. Frequently, we have resolved spelling puzzles by referring to the travel guide *Bhutan,* by the noted scholar Francoise Pommaret. The Bhutanese spell things (including their own names) every which way, and they do not waste much time worrying about it.

The voice in this book is primarily "we." It is an unusual pronoun for book writing, but these are "we stories." We cannot imagine having embarked on this adventure (or the last 38 years of our lives) without the advice and support of each other. Occasionally, we tell a story that relates to just one of us. Examples can be found in the sketches "Learning the Ropes" and "Ha Dzongda's Brother."

Enjoy!

Druk

The druk (dragon) is Bhutan's national symbol. One encounters the druk at every turn—painted on walls, carved in wood, and printed at the top of letterheads.

The Consequence of Ridges

Bhutan reminds of us of Vida, Oregon. Our hometown has a store, gas station, two eateries, and a post office. If you sneeze, you might miss it. But the terrain takes your breath away. The forest and river and mountains have a power that makes human beings seem like inconsequential visitors.

In a similar way, Bhutan is, on most maps of Asia, just a speck—too small to encompass the country's name within the boundaries. You might notice a blob between India and Tibet. The country is actually the size of Switzerland, but sandwiched between Methuselahs, Bhutan seems like a printer's error.

On topographic maps, Bhutan will be a patch of ground on the south slope of the Himalayas. The lower edge merges into the Indian plain, at about 300 feet elevation. The country then rises in stomach-lurching jumps until it reaches 26,000 feet along the Tibetan border. The topographic contours show a succession of steep ridges and narrow river valleys. The term "arable land" seems inapplicable here.

Maps do not explain why people have elected to live in this place. Unifying a country, or even getting to know your neighbors, would be heavy enterprises. Growing enough to eat would be a relentless problem. Winter weather and unstable mountain terrain would make life short and hard.

The truth is that not many did choose to live here—or perhaps more accurately, not many survived long enough to be included in a head count. Six hundred thousand seems to be the most popular number for the country's current population, although counting people in this terrain is iffy. Bhutan is not a crowded place; it seems more like Montana than the Boston/New York corridor. The Bhutanese are fond of saying that their country is the only nation in Southeast Asia that is underpopulated.

If we could transport you at this moment to the capital city of Thimphu, you might declare that all Bhutanese look the same: robust, self-confident, handsome people, almost all of them wearing the national dress. Aha, you would say. This tiny part of the world is an enclave, home to a tribe of people with the same features, language, and customs.

You would be wrong. Bhutan is a kaleidoscope. It is the perfect place to study what happens to cultures when they are shaped by ridges.

Technically, we regard most people in Bhutan as Mongoloid in their origins. In the southern part of the country, there are people who fall into the category of Indo-Aryan. Those labels, however, give not a hint of the country's human diversity.

Imagine taking a brush and painting a streak across the middle belt of Bhutan, from west to east. You will have highlighted the parts of Bhutan where human life is easiest. (Remember, though, that in this part of the world, "easy" is relative.) The Bhutanese often call this region the "central valleys." True enough, there are valleys here, but what you will really notice are relentless, heartbreakingly steep ridges.

Many of the people who live in the central valleys of Western Bhutan speak a Tibeto-Burman language called Dzongkha. Bhutan's government has made Dzongkha the national language. It is slow going. Many Bhutanese prefer their own dialects (which are often unrelated to Dzongkha) and English. Dzongkha is unsuited for modern concepts, especially technical ones. Do a little eavesdropping in Bhutan, and you will constantly hear conversations in Dzongkha that go something like this (where "X" equals words of Dzongkha): "X hard drive X 20 percent off X great deal."

In the middle of Bhutan, there is a mountain range known as the Black Mountains. Here, Bhutan's geography changes from challenging to nearly hopeless (at least from the point of view of a flatlander). And diversity in language and culture becomes head spinning.

Only a masochist would want to know the names of all the languages spoken in Central and Eastern Bhutan. Just to get the flavor of it, here are some of them: Nyenkha, Lakha, Brokkat, Olekha, Bumthangkha, Tsangmakha, Chalikha, Khengkha, Gongdupekha, Tshangla, Dzalakha, and Brokpakhe.

Cultures in the central valleys are similarly diverse. Some people live in the bottoms of valleys, others live on the tops of ridges. Some raise yaks, others are farmers. Some migrate seasonally, and others stay put. Each microregion has its own mountain deities, making human life either miserable or tolerable, depending on when you ask.

But is formal Buddhism a remarkable exception to Bhutan's diversity? Has Buddhism created a social fabric that, in the end, is more powerful and impressive than differences in language and ways of life? And are the Bhutanese themselves fond of describing their country as a Buddhist kingdom, above all else?

Well, yes and no. For the last 1,000 years, the Buddhism practiced in Bhutan has been divided into a number of schools, which until modern time were literally warring factions. In today's Bhutan, Buddhism is still divided between two orders (Kagyu and Nyingma) that have somewhat distinct rituals and deities.

More important, the daily lives of Bhutanese people are not exclusively rooted in Buddhism. Instead, the people often place their bets on ancient deities and shamanic practices, which frequently have a Buddhist patina but are in reality microreligions. The local deities are different from each other, valley to valley. They have been influenced by ridges. (See the sketches "The Spirits Within" and "What Do Monks Do?".)

Kings, however, may be the most interesting consequence of ridges. On December 17, 1907, a powerful local leader named Ugyen Wangchuck became the first king of modern Bhutan. A hereditary monarchy took root, which has now produced four kings, all of them remarkable human beings. These men have been blessed with wisdom, strength, vision, and selfless behavior. We are not sure if Bhutan shaped them or if they shaped Bhutan, or both. But we daydream about the United States borrowing the current king, just for a while. We could use the tutorial.

What do ridges have to do with kings? We have never heard anybody say this, but we believe that ridges, in part, created the political environment that made kings, or their equivalent, necessary.

To get the point, you will need to imagine Bhutan in ancient times. In its early history, Bhutan was the place "over there." Tibetans viewed Bhutan as a hidden and mysterious place. Little is known about the religion of the time, but it is often described as a combination of animism and shamanism. Although ancient Bhutan had several names (our favorite is "The Southern Land of Medicinal Herbs"), it had no political coherence.

Buddhism reached Bhutan shortly after it arrived in Tibet—according to tradition, around the 7th century A.D. From then until the 16th century, Bhutan was a fertile place for Tibetan missionaries seeking to expand the power of various competing schools of Tibetan Buddhism. Their fortunes ebbed and flowed, and little Bhutan continued to struggle along without a shred of political unity.

A momentous thing happened in the 17th century. A man known as the "Shabdrung" fled Tibet, landed in Western Bhutan, became a genius at overcoming his opponents, and accumulated power. Western people tend to see Buddhism as withdrawn from politics, but the Shabdrung's story shows that Buddhists can achieve political power as vigorously as anyone. (The history of Tibet proves the same thing.)

The Shabdrung built a chain of fortresses called *"dzongs"*—magnificent buildings for which Bhutan is famous. He defeated five invasions from Tibet and struggled incessantly and successfully against competing schools of Buddhism within Bhutan. By the time of his death in 1651, Western Bhutan had been unified, and shortly afterward, Central and Eastern Bhutan had been brought under centralized control as well.

Visit Bhutan in the 21st century and you will instantly see the challenges confronting the Shabdrung. Even today, this place has the most difficult travel conditions you will ever encounter. Now, there is a tiny road that connects Bhutan, west to east. But in the Shabdrung's time, it took weeks, traveling on astonishingly arduous and primitive trails, to cover the same distance.

The Shabdrung installed a complicated and comprehensive system of government that divided power among religious and civilian hierarchies, tied together by a strong person at the top. Naturally, it all fell apart after the Shabdrung died. The problem of ridges took over, and Bhutan returned to nonstop power struggles and civil wars. Finally, by 1905 Ugyen Wangchuck managed to struggle back to a power position similar to that of the Shabdrung 200 years earlier.

In 1907, the religious and lay leaders of Bhutan, exhausted by conflict and bloodshed, elected Ugyen Wangchuck the first king of Bhutan. The British, who ruled India at the time, had a significant (although behind the scenes) role in bringing the first king to power, since they preferred to deal with a single authority in a region they considered a buffer. A period of enormous progress in every dimension commenced. Bhutan became a stable, peaceful place in which unique experiments in the balancing of spiritual and material growth could be attempted. Thanks to its kings, Bhutan, for only the second time in its recorded history, had coped with the issue of ridges.

Riddles Lie Here

There is a theme about human development you might encounter. It goes something like this: "When a society is fortunate to have abundant resources, such as arable land and water, the people will have some spare time. They can then turn their attention to magnificent buildings and elaborate religious practices." This is the view of life you might hear expressed at the Egyptian pyramids, or the Hindu complexes of Bali, or the sprawling temples of Angkor Wat.

Bhutan, however, is different. This is a great place for flora and fauna, but it is harsh indeed for people. Farmable land comes in tiny patches, most of them carved out of the sides of mountains. Crops are constantly raided by monkeys and wild boars. Even if a farmer manages to grow a little surplus, the rough terrain cuts him off from marketplaces.

Yet Bhutan has both an elaborate religion and magnificent buildings. This plucky group of men and women has beat the odds.

In this sketch, we consider the buildings. And what buildings they are. Architecture is the first thing that most visitors notice when they arrive. The buildings are robust, handsome, and ornate. They are martial and spiritual all at once. They are out of scale to the tiny population and its humble resources.

You start to get hints about architecture as your plane winds down the canyons in its stomach-churning approach to the Paro Airport. The plane banks to the right, and there, just a few hundred yards from the wing tip, are astonishingly handsome farm buildings, perched on slopes that look fine for goats but not for human beings. Another maneuver, and the same thing.

When you have landed and looked around, you see an imposing building on a hill. The Paro Dzong, someone says, and above it, the watch tower. ("*Dzong*" can be roughly translated as "fortress.") If you are visiting in the spring, the Paro Dzong is framed by fields of yellow flowers in the front, snow-covered mountains behind, and the intense blue of a high-altitude sky above. You may hear the wispy sound of chanting, bells, and drums, carried by the wind from far away. You have arrived, the *dzong* says, at an uncommon place.

If you have sharp eyes, other remarkable things come into view. The Paro Valley is surrounded by serious mountains (in a short while, you will find that you can say this about any place in Bhutan). On the tops of ridges, in every direction, you see tiny buildings, utterly cut off from farmland, streams, shelter, and the other comforts of life. You learn that these are *gompas* (monasteries), *lhakhangs* (temples), and *chortens* (smaller buildings that honor famous lamas or scare away evil spirits). In your mind's eye, you envision the men and women who built these places. You catch a glimpse of sacrifice, tenacity, and, above all, imagination without limit.

We need to get our heads out of the clouds and take a more orderly look at the architecture of Bhutan. The place to start is the *dzong*. *Dzongs* (introduced in the preceding sketch) are found throughout Bhutan, often located on strategic hilltops. Most of them are massive complexes, with sloped walls, ornate woodwork, and pitched roofs. They often have a central courtyard and a tower in the middle. *Dzongs* house both monastic communities and civilian leaders.

Dzongs were built for exactly the same reason that castles and fortresses were built in other parts of the world—to consolidate power and control. They are peaceful, benign places now, but for a long time *dzongs* were centers of unrelenting struggles for dominion.

Dzongs have set the style in Bhutan. *Gompas, lhakhangs,* and even farmhouses tend to look like small, less militaristic *dzongs*. Even in modern times, new architectural themes in rebuilt *dzongs* (like the Thimphu and Punakha Dzongs) have swept through the country, altering new construction in both rural and "urban" places.

When you become more familiar with architecture in Bhutan, the real marvel will strike you. It is not the imposing *dzongs*, not the busy *gompas*, and not the ethereally beautiful *lhakhangs*. It is the farmhouses.

Why farmhouses? More than any other building, they illustrate our point about the disconnect between resources and architectural grandeur. The typical Bhutanese farmhouse is built at the edge of a modest farming enterprise. Patches here and there, and that is it. You can imagine these plots sustaining a family for a month or two, but not much longer.

And what kind of housing would this lilliputian farm support? In any other part of the world, a dwelling much less imposing.

But these houses are literally monumental. They are two or three stories tall. Walls are massive, built from stone or tamped earth. Weighty, hand-hewn timbers form the interior frames and floors. Window frames are complex shapes, covered with carvings and painted floral and geometric designs. The best room of the house is the altar room, which is decorated with the Bhutanese passion for color, texture, and shape. In traditional times, all of this was accomplished without a single nail.

If the land has been inhabited for multiple generations, you might also find the hulks of abandoned houses slowly merging back into the land. Some Bhutanese farmhouses, notwithstanding their scale and strength, only last for the lifetime of untreated wood. Therefore, on a regular basis, farmhouses must be rebuilt in their entirety. Again, the question—how can a small population, with practically no resources, do this?

The answer could be twofold. Farmland in Bhutan is scarce, but the things from which farmhouses are made—earth, stone, and timber—are abundant. The more important part of the answer might be human. Especially in modern times, Bhutanese country people cooperate. Farmhouses are not built by a family alone. Instead, practically everyone in the region pitches in.

On page 89 of this book, we include a painting of the Four Friends. They achieved wonderful things by cooperating, accomplishments that none of them could have done by themselves. You will encounter the Four Friends at every turn in Bhutan. Without doubt, the value of cooperation is uppermost in the minds of Bhutanese people. Farmhouses can be seen as dramatically tangible proof of Four Friends morality.

We, however, are not entirely satisfied by our Western "let's count the reasons" explanation. We have spent enough time in Bhutan to know that there is more than meets the eye. There is an element of miracle in Bhutanese architecture that cannot be shoved into four-corner reasoning. And that is the long and short of it.

To Ha, the End of the Sky

Most visitors to Bhutan fall in love with the Bhutanese people. It happens to all of us, whether we are young or old, tenderhearted or hard-boiled. We come home talking about mountains, rivers, *dzongs*, and wall art, but most of all, we talk about Kinga, and Tenzin, and Tshering, and all the other remarkable people we encountered.

In part, it is physical. These are handsome people—lean, sculpted, and erect, with smiles that would win awards anywhere on earth. When Bhutanese men and women put on their best *ghos* and *kiras*, the human form is pushed to its highest plane. By comparison, we Westerners, with earth-tone clothing and pale skins, look rudimentary.

In greater part, it is behavioral. Although these generalities do not always hold true, they are often visible. Bhutanese people are courtly—to you, and among themselves. They are self-confident without being pushy. They are soft-spoken, kindly people, but they know how to stand up for themselves when they need to. Bhutanese have a great sense of humor, which is frequently ribald in just the right ways.

Like all love stories, this one becomes more complex as it deepens. In important ways, the Bhutanese and Western personas are utterly different. Sometimes the differences are exasperating, in both directions.

There is an elderly gentleman in Bhutan who is a prototype of Bhutanese sensibilities: Shingkhar Lam Kungzang Wangchuck—raised in a village, trusted colleague of two kings, Speaker of the National Assembly, and lama. In this sketch we will dwell on snippets of Shingkhar Lam's life, because they are interesting episodes in their own right, and because they will give you solid insights on the interior lives of Bhutanese people.

These days, Shingkhar Lam's name is preceded by the honorific title of "Dasho." Although our sketch does not use the title, you may mentally add it to his name.

Shingkhar Lam was raised in the 1930s and 1940s, during the reign of the second king (Jigme Wangchuck, who reigned until 1952). His family was prominent religiously, but otherwise very poor. They had tiny herds of cattle, yaks, and sheep, a crumbling three-story house, and a license to collect alms in neighboring villages. Shingkhar Lam's father paid his taxes in kind by performing Buddhist rituals in the nearby temples of Kurje and Jakar.

Wolves, tigers, and leopards roamed the mountain ranges above Shingkhar Lam's village. All travel took place on "mule tracks"—loads were carried primarily by people and secondarily by animals. Food was precious, scarce, and simple. Even the best food items were spartan by our standards: dried pumpkin and radish, buckwheat flour, rice, maize, mushrooms, cheese, eggs, and dried meat.

Most of the people in Shingkhar Lam's village had never traveled beyond their region. In their eyes, the edges of Bhutan were astonishingly remote. The little town of Ha, along Bhutan's western border, must have seemed like a different planet. The people had Tibetans living among them and knew a thing or two about India, but the rest of the world was invisible. Indeed, there were no roads at all connecting Bhutan with any other country.

Health care was minimal. For example, in the summer of 1949, an epidemic sprang forth in the village of Shingnyer, in the district of Bumthang. The second king wanted to provide the village with medical help, but there was nothing he could do. In the entire country, there was only a poorly equipped hospital in Ha and several "compounders" elsewhere in the country, who might have known more about castrating animals than treating humans. In the end, the only things the king could do for Shingnyer were to enforce a quarantine, provide food, and assist with the harvest.

Although money existed, barter was more important. Most people paid their taxes in kind—especially with cloth and labor. When lamas and nobles visited the second king, they always brought cloth and a pitcher of *ara* (a distilled grain spirit).

A form of involuntary (more or less) servitude was practiced in the days of Shingkhar Lam's youth. The English word commonly used in Bhutan for these people is "serfs." Serfs were finally given their freedom in 1958.

It seems astonishing that a person who is alive today could have experienced such things in his youth. In Western culture, you would have to reach back to the Middle Ages to find comparable settings. But in Bhutan, many living people have shared Shingkhar Lam's experience; they were raised in circumstances that were, by Western standards, practically medieval.

It is true that present-day villages have better health care, education, and transportation. Nevertheless, for Bhutanese who are thirty years of age and older, the villages of their youth were virtually the same as those in which Shingkhar Lam lived. By any standard, they were breathtakingly isolated. It was a rough, risky life in which little was logical or sequential, and spirits, often unruly and malicious, ruled every moment of every day.

The men and women you meet on the streets of Thimphu (the capital) are frequently educated, urbane, and fluent in English. However, their inner selves are shaped by the survival lessons taught in tiny villages in Himalayan valleys and ridge tops. You will probably not sense the many-sided makeup of these people when you know them superficially. But get to know the Bhutanese better, and you increasingly come to understand that they come from two different realms.

Americans especially, with their straight-ahead and linear style of life, may not be prepared for the interior facets of the Bhutanese character. And there may be some misunderstanding in the opposite direction. No matter how hard they try, Bhutanese people may not entirely comprehend what it is like to live on other side of the world, in an environment where most of us have never faced a bleak shortage of food, walked three days to reach the nearest road, or met a spirit face-to-face.

When Shingkhar Lam was about 14, life took a turn. His uncle, who had been an attendant in the second king's court, suddenly disappeared. The king had sent the uncle to India to buy provisions. The uncle never returned and was deemed to be in default of his service obligation to the king. The next of kin were automatically held responsible. Shingkhar Lam and his brother were conscripted by the king to serve as lowly retainers in payment for their uncle's infidelity. For decades afterward, Shingkhar Lam worked for the country's kings and oligarchy.

It was a stern existence. Many of the king's attendants lived only on buckwheat flour. Shingkhar Lam was slightly better off, receiving rice, wheat flour, butter, a few dried chilies, and a roll of dry meat. Although Shingkhar Lam had a few trappings of a personal life (including a number of wives), there was no question that he served his superiors morning, noon, and night. Even though he was respected for his literary abilities and his knowledge of Bhutanese culture, he was subject to the decisions and whims of his masters. Even small errors brought immediate, corporal punishment.

For example, one of Shingkhar Lam's boyhood jobs was to keep a record of food consumption in the royal community. One day, he was unable to make the usual entries in the register because the register was kept in a room behind the king's wooden tub (which the king was occupying). When the king asked if the day's entries had been made, Shingkhar Lam, in a moment of panic, told a fib. When the king discovered that the register was in fact incomplete, he sentenced Shingkhar Lam to a beating. A senior attendant lashed Shingkhar Lam with a whip, with all his force.

In a similar episode, Shingkhar Lam once visited a friend late at night. Unfortunately, the king decided that night to have Shingkhar Lam read a few episodes from the *Epic of Gesar*. The next morning, Shingkhar Lam was whipped with peach branches until he convulsed and fell unconscious.

These experiences suggest some important points about verticality in Bhutanese society. Living in Bhutan meant, and still means, living in a hierarchy, both religious and civilian. It is a land of pecking orders in which the gradations are taken seriously. The first thing that happens when Bhutanese enter a temple is prostration, with foreheads knocking on wooden floors. Everyone has an acute sense of personal space, and the people maintain a carefully calculated distance from those on a higher plane. When an ordinary citizen encounters a prominent lama, he covers his mouth (to avoid polluting the exalted person) and bows his head.

A sense of hierarchy has its virtues. Old people are often venerated. Teachers are admired. Children do not have foul and disrespectful mouths. Kings are held in high esteem. When the kings also happen to be wise men and extraordinarily committed to the community, the results are spectacular.

When we are working in Bhutan, we usually take a walk in the early morning. Our ventures overlap the time in which the children are walking to school. "Good morning sir, good morning madam," they all say, perfectly dressed in their *kiras* and *ghos*. We would cheerfully take each and every one home with us. Morning after morning, we fall in love with Bhutanese children.

There is another reality at work here. The hierarchy pays dividends for the Bhutanese, but it also carves out a gap between us and them. Until we went to work in Bhutan, we did not fully realize it, but Americans are egalitarian to their bones. There are aspects of the verticality in Bhutanese society that make us grit our teeth. Too frequently, we see superiors who are not kind, gracious, or attentive to their inferiors. Officials are the object of bowing and scraping, whether they are competent or not. This goes on in both religious and secular settings.

It is an odd situation. Behaviors like these would be intolerable if they occurred at home. Even in Bhutan, they are disconcerting. We realize that we are stuck in an oscillation—uncomfortable with the hierarchy at one moment, realizing that it is often the right thing for the Bhutanese people at the next.

The second king of Bhutan died in 1952. Shingkhar Lam resigned from the court and went home—but he did not remain a homebody for long. By 1955, Shingkhar Lam was in Thimphu, the newly established capital of Bhutan, working for the third king. Bhutan was beginning to open to the outside world, especially India. Prime Minister Nehru visited Bhutan in 1958, and the Bhutanese reciprocated with a visit to India in the next year. In 1962, a road was constructed between Thimphu and the Indian border. Prime Minister Indira Gandhi visited the country in 1968, and Bhutanese people attended Expo '70 in Osaka, Japan. Shingkhar Lam (who in 1968 had become Secretary to the king) was an important participant in all of these country-altering events.

In 1971, Shingkhar Lam became the Speaker of the National Assembly. He had emerged as the prototype Bhutanese, with a perfectly balanced set of skills: courtly behaviors, sensitivity to Bhutanese culture, and mastery of Tibetan Buddhist beliefs. Listen to these words about Shingkhar Lam, written by our friend Karma Ura:

> When he spoke, his upper frame was stooped forward in a position of courtesy and attentiveness, and he spoke in a soft tone. His delicate manner of speech was inimitable, even though some tried to imitate him. The closely-

cropped head, which is so typical of the Bhutanese, brought out the contours of his oval shaped head and somehow heightened the entrenched impression of his modesty and sensibility that prevailed. He spoke always in a low tone and sounded in a peculiar way both grave and graceful. It was the voice of a man who had witnessed events from a broader perspective of having a thousand eyes, and whose views were tempered by the middle path. He took everything seriously in spite of realizing the cosmic unimportance of every event.[1]

This paragraph resonates for us like no other. We are not certain that any of the Bhutanese we know incorporate all of these qualities at once. But there is no doubt in our minds that many Bhutanese strive earnestly to model their daily lives after Shingkhar Lam. Each phrase in Karma Ura's summation makes us say, "Ah yes, there is Sonam, or Yangzom, or Jigme."

And that is why so many Western people feel powerful bonds with the citizens of Bhutan. We may analyze this, or quibble about that, but in the end our inner voices are telling us that the people of this Himalayan kingdom are plainly different from the rest of us. We catch glimpses of human potential, and we are captured by them.

An Enterprise of Polarities

The Bhutanese love a good time, but traditionally the travails of a harsh climate, rigorous geography, and hard-scrabble farms have not left much room for diversions. Thus, sporting and recreational opportunities are treasured.

Archery is the ideal example. It is the national sport and in many ways the perfect metaphor of Bhutanese culture. Like so many other aspects of life in Bhutan, archery is replete with polarities. It is a martial art in a country that abhors killing. It is gripping for Bhutanese people but moves at an excruciatingly slow pace. It is a sport dominated by modern compound bows but at every turn is shaped by ancient attitudes towards spirits, auspicious signs, and ceremony.

Two wooden rectangular targets are set up at the ends of a long field. The targets are small (3 feet tall and 11 inches wide), and the field is alarmingly long (460 feet, or the length of one and a half football fields). At first glance, most Westerners feel that bows cannot shoot arrows far enough to hit the target. They can, but hitting the target is quite a challenge, especially if the light is bad or the wind is blowing.

Each team has thirteen players. The teams take turns shooting from one end of the field (with each player shooting two arrows) and then take turns shooting from the other end. The first team to get 25 points wins. Because of some complications in the scoring system, winning can take a long time.

In earlier times, an archery tournament could last a month or more. Bhutanese archery moves at a quicker pace now, but it is still glacial by Western standards. Soon, you discover that it is not the game itself that provides the most interesting action. Bhutanese archery can be seen as the nominal focal point for a large-scale party.

There are two kinds of archery matches. In a traditional match, the players use bamboo bows (made from either a single piece of bamboo or two pieces held together by iron bands). Traditional arrows are also made of bamboo, and the vanes actually come from birds. In a modern match, players use compound bows that are imported from the West. The arrows (also imported) are made of aluminum; the vanes are plastic.

Traditional archery has an entirely different kind of rhythm from its modern counterpart. With a traditional bamboo bow, the player pulls back the bowstring until he is almost at the limit of his strength. He has only a second or two to take aim and release. Often the arrow is sent on its way with a snap. With modern compound bows, the pressure "lets off" as the shooter pulls back the string. When the player is at full draw, he is only holding about half the peak weight. He can take his time, aim carefully, and release in a smooth, fluid way.

The majority of Bhutanese archers love compound bows because they are comfortable and accurate. But the Bhutanese probably have a sense of regret, knowing that sooner or later the compounds will overpower traditional archery. In fact, it is already happening. Modern tournaments are now more popular than traditional ones. We once expressed an interest in buying an authentic traditional bow and set of arrows but discovered that the real things seldom appear in the Thimphu market. A villager can have a bow made by a local expert; otherwise this ancient craft might be disappearing.

Bhutanese archery is a martial art, reaching back to the days when a bow was the principal weapon in defending city states and fighting off Tibetan invaders. Perhaps this the reason that the shooting distance in the modern sport is so long. Four hundred and sixty feet might have been the greatest distance, more or less, at which a bow and arrow could cause damage.

In modern times, archery has altogether lost its military character. Bows and arrows are not used in Bhutan for hunting (which would violate the Buddhist prohibition against killing sentient beings). They are used only for target matches, which are amiable community events at which everyone has a good time.

You will encounter Bhutanese archery again in other sketches, where it becomes an ideal microscope for examining the Bhutanese sense of humor and the practical role of local deities. For now, we ask you to envision archery as a complex and deeply rewarding community event.

Imagine a sunny, sparkling day in late November. You are in Paro Valley, in the western part of Bhutan. At every turn, the valley presents scenes of beauty that bring a lump to your throat: snow-covered peaks of the high Himalayas, tiny meditation huts clinging to ledges in rock walls, prayer flags moving gently in the morning air. The dense green of forest fills in spaces between rock and river and sky. In your mind's eye, you sense Guru Rinpoche riding on the back of his tiger to this valley, subduing demons and meditating for months in a cave you can almost see from here, at a place called the Tiger's Lair.

Two archery teams have gathered on Ugyen Rinzin's land in the western part of the valley. Thirteen players represent Ha, a seldom-visited region in the far west of the country. Another thirteen represent Yangphel Travel, one of the better teams from the capital city of Thimphu. The match has just begun.

The governor of Ha has, as usual, recruited the best players for his team. They are excited and a little scared about facing a team of polished players from Thimphu. They hoped they could play on their home field, but the game shifted to Paro (to the east of Ha) at the last minute.

As he moves among his team, the governor is jolly at one moment, a little stern the next. He will play on the team himself, but the governor shoots a bow the way he negotiates life—full of energy and bravado. He will depend on his more deliberate shooters to rack up the score.

Eight women have accompanied the team from Ha. Their job spans an astonishing range: dancing and singing in traditional ways, presenting the latest love songs, cheering on some of the players, and dishing out spur-of-the-moment insults to the others. As the women move among the crowd, their *kiras* make a quilt of radiant colors. Ancient melodies sound in the morning air, reminding us that archery has been at the foundation of Bhutanese life since the beginning of recorded history.

A canopy has been set up in the center of the field. In a formal match, it would be a formidable structure, covered with Bhutanese symbols. In this case, it is on a more humble scale, but still a comfortable place. People scurry around, preparing the food and drink that will keep the players happy all day long. Soon, both sides of the field are filled with spectators. Word has spread around this end of the valley, and no one wants to miss the show.

Thwock! The sound of an arrow hitting the soft pine target delights the crowd. In one ear, you hear male voices singing in celebration. In the other, seeming like a kind of stereo, are the sounds of the women's traditional songs. Old folks chat with their friends, children raise their voices in play, men and women joke and laugh and chatter among their peers. The sound of a human community, brought together by archery, drifts into Paro Valley, filling it with the sheer joy of living on a beautiful day.

Learning the Ropes

An archery match was under way on a misty, summer day in the little town of Ha. Rain was threatening, and the players lit a pile of juniper branches at the end of the field, hoping to persuade the local deities to drive away the rain. Smoke spread gently through the air.

We had spent the night in a guest house. Before we went to bed, the caretaker asked us if we wanted "bed tea." We said yes, with no clue about what we had agreed to. We crept around and found one of our Bhutanese friends, who explained that the caretaker would bring us tea in the morning, before we were out of bed. And so he did.

The match was spectacular. The high school girls doing the dancing and teasing were a bright and cheerful bunch. In his usual jovial way, the governor of Ha kept the food and drinks arriving all day long. Male and female voices made a joyful sound, celebrating hits, teasing players, cracking jokes. Then, the propitious words were spoken. Russ, you can do this! Play archery with us during your next trip. Come on—you can do it!

I had played target archery once, in the Boy Scouts. That was a long time ago. But this seemed like a once-in-a-lifetime chance, so I said yes.

After returning home, the first step was to buy a bow. I decided to buy a Hoyt bow (made in the U.S.) from the only archery dealer in Bhutan. (Buying from a dealer half a world away is not the usual method, but I wanted to give the business to someone in Bhutan.) The bow was delivered by UPS to our home in Oregon, so the whole thing worked seamlessly. For the first time in 35 years, I held a target bow in my hands and wondered: can I hit anything at all with this?

To accompany this beautiful new bow, I needed to buy arrows and the usual archery accessories. I was insecure and went to both archery stores in Eugene looking for a consultant. Can you help me, I asked. I'll be participating in tournaments in the country of Bhutan. They shoot at wooden targets 11 inches wide, at a distance of 460 feet.

Keep in mind that this part of the Pacific Northwest is still serious hunting country. In the opinions of most archers here, bows and arrows are meant for four-footed animals (mainly deer and elk), not little pieces of wood. During part of the year, the locals might shoot at "3-D" imitations of animals, but only to get ready for the real thing. The longest distance in a 3-D tournament is normally 150 feet. Four hundred and sixty feet might as well be 460 miles.

Then there was the matter of Bhutan. My consultant candidates had a mild curiosity, but no passionate interest, in this distant Himalayan country. After a couple of weeks, I gave up the search for a local adviser.

I turned to mail-order catalogs. Reading the captions in a catalog is not the best way to get updated on the sport of archery, but it worked (more or less). Slowly, making all the mistakes of a beginner, I found the equipment and learned the basics of target-archery technique.

Many of the basics, however, are designed for shooting at less than half the distance of Bhutanese archery. So I had to experiment, developing my own, and no doubt highly flawed, methods for shooting an arrow so far that it disappears from sight before it lands.

My first chance to shoot in Bhutan occurred during a trip whose primary purpose was to work on computer issues. A few days after my arrival, Sonam Jatso and I went to an informal archery range to take some warm-up shots.

In Bhutanese archery, each player shoots two arrows per round. Sonam and I each took two shots at the target. The first thing I discovered is that if the light is dim or if the background is jumbled, the target virtually disappears. I squinted at a tiny, amorphous smudge of white and let fly. Whack! We both looked astonished. I shot a second time. Whack—a double! To me, it seemed I might be making some progress in my spiritual development after all. To Sonam, it must have seemed like a miscarriage of justice.

You already know the rest of this story. It is what always happens to beginners. I labored hard after those first two shots, but it was a long time before I hit the target again.

The morning after the Archery Miracle, we found out that word had already spread through Thimphu. (There's a big Western guy practicing archery. He can actually hit the target.) I began to understand that this archery experiment, which at the beginning had seemed like a private experience between me and some of my friends, would become a community event.

A nervous feeling began to grow deep in the stomach. Then the nightmares set in. Each night, I dreamt about the Bhutanese spectators crowded around the target. Each night, one of my shots went awry. For the rest of the night I imagined being the first Western person in history to shoot a Bhutanese.

In Bhutan, a grim frame of mind does not last long. The good humor and generosity of the people soon recharge your spirits. I cheerfully practiced each afternoon and slowly got the hang of it. Without fail, I forgot that Bhutanese archers play for money during their practice sessions. I arrived at the practice field broke. During the match, I realized that losing would have embarrassing consequences. But one thing I am good at is running scared. So I, fearful of looking like a deadbeat, practiced as if my life depended on it.

Over time, I played in a series of games, ranging from pickup matches to real tournaments. The first time I shot reasonably well was in a tournament against the police team. The teams were evenly matched, with the lead oscillating back and forth. In this game, there were no women to take care of the teasing, so the opposing team members did it themselves.

You could tell that they were not quite sure how to tease a Westerner. They tried general-purpose harassment, without result. Then they tried the usual run of insults. But I had not suffered through law school for nothing. Finally, one of the senior members of the police team waited until I was at full draw. He dropped to his and knees, crawled up to me, looked up my *gho,* and announced to the crowd at full voice: "He doesn't have one!" Outwardly, I did not move a muscle. But inside, a thousand voices were laughing.

Now, we transport ourselves to the town of Mongar, in Eastern Bhutan. An archery match is under way; the Education Department is playing a team from the village of Tangmachu.

Like other towns in the east, Mongar is built on the top of a ridge. The valleys in this part of Bhutan are narrow and steep; practically no one can live along the rivers at the bottom. Instead, villages are carved out of slopes and mountaintops. Mongar's archery field is on the edge of cliffs. It is a handsome place, with views that extend to the edge of Tibet.

The players from the Education Department are teachers at the high school in Mongar. Quiet, studious souls, they have that earnest look shared by teachers the world around. Tangmachu's players are farmers and shopkeepers, jolly and earthy. It all seems normal, except that I have joined the team from Tangmachu. This seems to be the first time in Mongar's history that a Westerner has played archery here. The children of Mongar are fascinated and follow me wherever I go, like an Asian version of the Pied Piper.

The field is crowded with people. Some watch every shot in the archery match, but many are here for a general-purpose good time. An impromptu soccer match springs up, right next to the shooting lane for the archers. Children are running in every direction. Some of them scoot right under arrows, which makes my heart lurch, but which seems perfectly normal to everyone else.

When the match is over, the players from Tangmachu are a little stunned to discover they have won. It is tough for country folk to beat players from a "downtown" place like Mongar. I am pleased, because I have had good luck and made a strong contribution to Tangmachu's victory.

As usual, the teams had a wager going. The Tangmachu players do not have much money and are visibly relieved to be on the receiving end.

In many cases, finishing a match like this is just the beginning of some serious partying. But the Tangmachu group has a long drive ahead, and the social component needs to be shortened. The Bhutanese instinct for gracious behavior takes over—soon the team members are exchanging courtesies, cracking jokes, and making wild claims about the next time they meet in archery.

Everyone goes home with a sense of kinship and warmth. I will never forget the gentle sportsmanship I found in that faraway place.

DRANGSONG

Drangsong is one of a multitude of local deities inhabiting the landscape. Local deities were at the heart of Himalayan religious practice before the arrival of Buddhism. Although many of them were "subdued" by Buddhist saints, local deities continue to occupy a central part of Bhutanese culture.

THE SPIRITS WITHIN

As a new day approaches, the night sky begins to lighten. You sense, but cannot see, the presence of enormous mountains along the horizon. A familiar shape begins to emerge, first wispy and indistinct, and then unmistakable, as the morning light gathers strength: Jichu Drake—the legendary mountain peak of Northwestern Bhutan. Sunlight catches the mountain's uppermost realms, altering them to brilliant gold. Light spreads down snow-covered slopes.

Jichu Drake dominates the horizon now. At this altitude, the terrain is a moonscape, without a sign of living things. The mountain's walls of rock and ice are untouchable and utterly remote from human affairs. Or so they seem.

In reality, Jichu Drake is a dwelling place. A mountain deity, also named Jichu Drake, lives there. Every other mountain peak in Bhutan is inhabited by a deity. In fact, all prominent features of the landscape—including lakes, rivers, and monolithic rocks—are occupied by a dizzying array of spirits. In Bhutan, even the air itself is a spirit world.

The favorite Western term for the Himalayan gods of geography is "sacred landscape." For a change, our terminology may get it right. This is a culture in which unseen forces, associated with the features of the land, are encountered at every turn. In Bhutan, there may be no such thing as an "inanimate object."

In this sketch, we use the term "local deities" to refer to the entire array of spirits connected to the landscape. When we use the phrase "Buddhist deities," we mean the equally huge number of deities that are associated explicitly with formal Buddhist practice and are not usually thought to dwell in any specific geographical feature.

Bhutanese people have coexisted with local deities since the beginning of recorded Himalayan history. You could describe the relationship between people and local deities as love/fear/respect. Local deities are loved because they are the source of daily good fortune and feared because they are also the source of periodic disaster. They are feared because of their capricious nature and, in the case of the uppermost deities, immense power. They are respected because in a risky place like the Himalayas, where human life hangs by a thread, people need all the supernatural help they can get.

When Buddhism arrived in the Himalayas, Buddhist "missionaries" needed to deal with a religion, based on local deities, that was powerful, complex, and pervasive. As opposed to some of the world's other great religions, which seem to have a history of wiping out indigenous practices, Buddhism has generally accommodated traditional beliefs, molding itself into a new school that blends the old and the new. According to Tantric Buddhist beliefs, each of the local deities in the region was confronted by Buddhist forces and "subdued." Indeed, the words "subdue" and "tame" arise over and over in the Tantric Buddhist tradition.

The champion tamer of local deities was a partly historic, partly mythic figure known as Guru Rinpoche. (He is also frequently referred to as "Padmasambhava," his Sanskrit name.) This remarkable man is venerated in Bhutan, and we will have many interesting things to say about him in later sketches. For now, it is enough to know that Guru Rinpoche brought Buddhism to Tibet and Bhutan in the 8th century. According to Buddhist tradition, Guru Rinpoche challenged and subdued one local deity after another, forcing all of them to swear an oath of allegiance to the new religion.

Guru Rinpoche's remarkable success emboldened other Buddhist priests to try the same thing. One of them, Terkungpa, had a famous encounter with a nasty local character named Godü Chenpo. The priest had been meditating on the shores of a lake when the deity suddenly emerged from the waters. He was quite a sight—huge, fat dribbling from his mouth, holding a bow and arrow in one hand and a snake in the other. The priest was unimpressed, which frustrated the local deity to no end. So the deity proposed a contest to find out which was more powerful. After introductory skirmishing, they agreed to swallow each other.

First, the priest swallowed the deity. When the deity reached the priest's midlevel interior, he decided to kill the priest by pulling on his intestines. But the priest was a crafty soul. He raised his body temperature, terrifying the local deity, who begged to be spat out.

Then the deity, who must have been a little dense, offered to swallow the priest. The priest proved that he could do on the inside the same thing he could do on the outside. He raised his body temperature, and the local deity writhed on the ground, nursing a monumental stomachache. The priest stopped the torture only when the deity agreed to subordinate himself to Buddhism.[2]

Another notable taming story involves two famous characters, one a Buddhist priest, the other a powerful local deity. The Buddhist was an entertaining and interesting character named Drukpa Kunley (who will be the subject of an entire sketch later in this book). The deity's name was Ödöpa, and to this day he is thought to inhabit a cave near Paro Valley.

Drukpa Kunley, being a fearless man, decided to spend the night in Ödöpa's cave. However, he did not prostrate himself or otherwise grovel in front of Ödöpa. Ödöpa was furious and mounted an attack. But Drukpa Kunley was too fast for him. He pinned Ödöpa down, removed the skin from Ödöpa's penis, and stuffed him in the skin, like a sack. When it rained, the sack expanded, but when the sun shone the sack contracted, leading to suffocation. Ödöpa remained in that condition for years. Finally, Drukpa Kunley returned to the cave and freed Ödöpa, but only after he had taken the usual oath to support Buddhism.[3]

Stories like these could go on forever. To our ears, however, they have the ring of wishful thinking. Local deities may now be official members of the Buddhist pantheon, but perhaps the people themselves interpret local deities as unruly, unpredictable, and Buddhist on the surface only.

Bhutanese, even many urbane ones, feel in their bones that local deities control day-to-day life. Formal Buddhism is the belief system that deals with the grand issues, like reincarnation and personal enlightenment. But if you want your crops to be successful or your children to pass their school exams, you appeal to the ancient gods that dwell in the landscape.

Listen to these words from a Bon text. ("Bon" is a curious term. It is the name of a modern religion but is also a term often used for the religion of pre-Buddhist Tibet. In this quotation, the thinking is universal, applying to both Bon and Buddhist practitioners.)

> If you fail to give milk-offerings and pure sacrificial cakes
> to the powerful lords of this world,

> If you do not ask them (for a set for) your palace of the
>   Blessed Ones,
>
> these powerful lords, the lords of the soil, the serpents and
>   the furies, are irascible, however much they may
>   protect the doctrine,
>
> However gentle their disposition, their lineage is still that
>   of the titans....
>
> You must give pleasure to the powerful ones of the phe-
>   nomenal world,
>
> and having made them happy, you can hold them to their
>   former vows....
>
> Thus happiness in phenomenal things depends on (the
>   lords of) the soil.
>
> Fertile fields and good harvests,
>
> extent of royal power and spread of dominion,
>
> although half (of such effects) is ordained by previous
>   actions,
>
> the other half comes from the lords of the soil.[4]

Another interesting example of the irascible, independent nature of local deities comes from the deity who opened this sketch, Jichu Drake. In 1983, an expedition climbed to the top of Jichu Drake (the mountain). According to the local people, Jichu Drake (the deity) became so angry that he punished the region with devastating hail. The people then appealed to the king, asking him to prohibit all climbing of the mountain. The king agreed, and since then, both Jichu Drake the mountain and Jichu Drake the deity have enjoyed splendid isolation.

Until now, this sketch has been concentrating on deities that live in mountains. But, as you know from our preamble, Himalayan Buddhist people believe that local deities inhabit every feature of the natural world. It turns out that local deities come in many forms. They are differentiated not only by the terrain they occupy, but also in their power, gender, and role.

You are not expected to memorize the little table that follows. Instead, the point is the intensity of these people's connection with the natural world. In the eyes of Himalayan Buddhists, every square inch of the physical world is infused with spirit forces, many of which can cause great harm. (This list is not exhaustive; there are many more spirits that share the world with the Bhutanese.)[5]

> *Lu*—aquatic deities who live in springs, lakes, and rivers. They are female and have a reptilian lower half and human upper half. You must be very careful around water. If you pollute or divert water, you risk the anger of the *lu*. They seek revenge by making you sick, especially with leprosy.
>
> *Nyen*—spirits who generally live in trees. Before cutting a tree, you need to consult your astrological almanac carefully. An angry *nyen* can cause many illnesses, including cancer. *Nyen* are usually yellow and green.
>
> *Sadag*—lords of the soil (see the Bon quote above). You can irritate them by plowing, building, or otherwise disturbing the earth.
>
> *Tsen*—spirits of the rocks, who are male and the spirits of fallen monks. A genuinely tamed *tsen* makes a fine protector of temples and monasteries. Offerings to them should be colored red.
>
> *Gyelpo*—deities who were evil kings and lamas in their former lifetimes. They are generally powerful mountain deities who are white and carry armor.
>
> *Düd*—heavy-duty nasty spirits. They are all black, and during their former lifetimes, they were vigorously opposed to Buddhist practice.
>
> *Mamo*—ferocious female deities. They are also black and serve as general-purpose representatives of natural forces, which can be enormously malicious when they are disturbed.
>
> *Za*—unpleasant deities related to the planets. They, like many other deities, can cause illness. Epilepsy appears to be their specialty.

Nödjin—deities that guard the natural riches of the soil. By and large, they seem amiable, being associated with prosperity and medicine.

Lha—white deities, which are friendly toward people.

The comparative importance of these deities seems to vary from place to place. And we doubt that all Bhutanese persons would classify them in exactly the same way. Nevertheless, the drift is clear. The landscape of Bhutan is alive. It is sometimes a benevolent environment, but is more frequently a risky one. We imagine that the people of Bhutan sleep with one eye open.

Over the course of our trips to Bhutan, we have begun to sense extra dimensions and meanings within the inanimate world. We have caught a glimpse, now and then, of the soul-shaping power of forests, rivers, rocks, and ice in the largest mountains on earth. It would be disrespectful to say that we have achieved the same sensitivity for the natural world as the Bhutanese, but, without doubt, we are now students traveling along the same pathway.

During our working sessions in Thimphu, we are always hungry for the back country. Once, we talked Sonam into arranging a trek to the Jimilangtsho lakes, which lie high in the mountains west of Thimphu. Be careful, everyone said. A spirit lives in those lakes, and she will cause you great harm if you displease her, especially if you go fishing. Well, fishing was exactly what we had in mind, and in our hard-boiled, Western way, we ignored the advice.

The day was glorious when we started the hike. We visited the magnificent Phajoding Monastery along the way, and as we took in the views from Phajoding, we felt pleased with ourselves. Great day, beautiful country, and fine fishing ahead!

The trail rose higher and higher. The forest turned to alpine flora. At a high pass, we stopped at a rock cairn. Cairns like this one always appear in mountain passes and are thought to be the dwelling places of local deities. It was a place demanding respect. We burned juniper branches, hoping for good weather and a rewarding trip.

The mountains, however, began to look bleak and forbidding. And then it began to rain. After six more hours slogging through rain and mud, we made it to Jimilangtsho. We crawled into our tent and spent the night listening to the rain and wind.

The next morning it was still raining, and the high country was covered with fog. Good morning, said our Bhutanese friend. Would you like to try some fishing? We thought we should at least see the lake, so we made our way through the gloom, down to the water's edge. And there, in that misty, surreal place, we felt an inner stirring. As blind as we might be to the messages of the natural world, we still felt an odd sense of linkage to the lake and to whatever might dwell within. "No," we said. "No fishing today."

To end this sketch on a cheerful note, we will tell you about the archery *chorten*. There are many local deities who can be hidden participants in archery matches, but our favorite is a goddess who lives in the Jaychu Maamom Chorten (near Thimphu), known popularly as the "archery *chorten*."

The way to the heart of this goddess is to show her some impressive male anatomy. Team members who feel they need supernatural help rush out to the *chorten* (frequently in the middle of a match), lift their *ghos,* and show the goddess their stuff. Assuming that the goddess is impressed, the team member takes a memento from the place, like a string or flower, and carries it back to the match. The goddess then allies herself with the team members, becoming a de facto part of the roster.

When we visited the *chorten*, there was a small, barred door blocking access to the goddess' chamber. The door was secured with a padlock. About 15 years ago, explained the caretaker, there was an important match between the army team and a village team. An army major secretly left the match and went to the *chorten* to pay his respects. He removed the statue of the goddess, hid it under his *gho*, and returned to the match.

The major's team began to play very well. The other team got worried and sent one of its players to the *chorten* to impress the goddess and take back some sign of her approval. He was shocked to find that the statue had been taken. After losing the match, the village team discovered that the statue had been stolen by the major. There was much commotion, and since then, the door to the statue's chamber has been locked.

In the years that have passed since our first visit to Bhutan, we have noticed inner transformations taking place. We live in a log house, next to a magnificent river in a Douglas fir forest. When we first moved here, these things were scenery. Now, the natural setting has taken on a complex and ineffable cast for us. We are not sure what is going on, but we think it might have something to do with the spirits within.

Ha Dzongda's Brother

Please imagine that you have put a map of Bhutan on the wall and thrown a dart to the left of center. It will land close to the town of Tongsa, which is famous for its immense *dzong* perched on the side of a ridge, guarding the valley. Practically every visitor to Bhutan goes there and is impressed.

I am overwhelmed by this place, too. The inner courtyard has a little stone wall along its outer edge. When you peer over the side, your stomach lurches at the sight of a drop off whose verticality seems unsustainable. Look toward the horizon, and a mosaic of valleys, ridges, mountain peaks, rivers, and cliffs, all embedded in a sky of alpine blue, makes you feel like one of the smaller particles in the cosmos.

Tongsa is gripping culturally as well. This place is the best possible portrait of a paradox you will encounter regularly in Bhutan. In recent centuries, Bhutan was dominated by struggles for power and dominion. As the finest example of a military construction in Bhutan, Tongsa Dzong captures this facet of Bhutanese life.

However, the *dzong* is also a sacred place, housing temples, monks, and all the other components of Buddhist religious practice. In turn, Tantric Buddhism is a religion that abhors, in the clearest possible terms, control, material things, and all the other "attachments" to which some Bhutanese civilians were apparently addicted.

If you travel in Bhutan with your senses alert, you will find yourself traversing the Tongsa paradox at every step.

In my eyes, Tongsa is notable for another reason, which would never be detected by the casual visitor. This place is the home of Jangchu, a humble, practically invisible man. In this sketch, I tell his story.

Jangchu is the brother of the former governor of Ha, and his acquaintances occasionally refer to him as "Ha Dzongda's brother." I will call him Ha Dzongda's brother in this sketch because, in Bhutan, kinship relationships might be the single most important dimension of life. One is, before all else, someone's parent, child, brother, sister, aunt, uncle, or cousin.

The second reason to use a contextual name for Ha Dzongda's brother is that actual names are hopelessly confusing. Bhutanese do not have family names, so names do not tell you who is associated with whom. Many names work equally well for a male or female; it is, therefore, important to listen carefully to the pronouns associated with a person. Furthermore, the supply of names is limited. There may be only 50 or so names in common use; if you refer to your friend as "Kinga," or even "Kinga Tshering," you will probably also have to explain just which Kinga you have in mind. All in all, contextual names are problem solving.

Ha Dzongda's brother grew up in a part of northeastern Bhutan that, by today's standards, was indescribably remote. He had practically no formal education. On the surface, he was an ordinary young man dealing with the day-to-day struggle of surviving on a minimalist farm.

Ha Dzongda's brother was not, however, ordinary at all. He had an astonishing ability to communicate with the spirit world. At first, his gift was amorphous and unpredictable, but it steadily became more focused. Ha Dzongda's brother has now reached his fifties, and he is at the height of his powers.

This man's story will give you a hint of one of the wonderful features of Tantric Buddhism. Subject to some important exceptions, this is a people's belief system. Lamas and monks have monopolistic control over certain aspects of the religion, but laypeople (and "in-between" people) enjoy powerful, flourishing influence over others. Just as traditional Buddhist deities share power with local deities, the formal religious hierarchy of Tantric Buddhism shares roles with a dizzying array of religiously astute citizens.

The names themselves paint a picture of a vibrant, top-to-bottom religious tradition. Consider these: folk shamans, spirit mediums, oracle priests, visionary bards, clairvoyants, finders of hidden treasures, and saintly madmen. Ha Dzongda's brother would probably be classified as a spirit medium. He is, however, not a common one. He is the best.

It is rare for Western people to see a spirit medium in action—their spirit encounters are embedded in Bhutanese culture and are not compatible with groups, tour schedules, or cameras. We have been present only once; it took years of patience and the ability to sit inscrutably in a corner of the room. I will take you there now.

Imagine a house in the capital city of Thimphu. It is a handsome place, recently built on a hill overlooking Memorial Chorten. Most Bhutanese people would be thrilled to live there.

But the inhabitants are unhappy with this house. One after another, they have fallen sick. In the West, we might think that they had experienced bad luck with viruses and bacteria. If an individual case of illness were sufficiently troubling, we would pay a visit to the physician, who would diagnose and treat a pathogen.

That is not how it works in Bhutan. Although Western medicine has its place, the people are likely to look at illness in a holistic sense. Their first question is not Which bug do I have? It is much more likely to be What has gone wrong with my environment, and, specifically, is a spirit angry with me?

The sick people living in that house were diagnosed in the traditional way. The culprit was found. A *lu* (water-oriented female deity) is living in the earth underneath the house. She is angry that the house has been built in her realm.

To put this in context, this is a sophisticated family; their house contains at least six state-of-the-art computers, connected with a custom-designed local area network. Many of the occupants have excellent educations and have traveled internationally. There is a television set on the third floor. The inhabitants sometimes know more about American popular culture than we do. Yet most of them are convinced that they are in trouble with a *lu*. Even the few who are a little doubtful about the *lu* feel that spiritual intervention would be a good insurance policy.

In one aspect, the inhabitants are lucky. They are all relatives of Ha Dzongda's brother and thus have access to the most powerful medicine the culture can offer. He is asked to visit the house and deal with the angry spirit.

Encounters with a local deity cannot happen at a moment's notice. In general, they should be attempted only on auspicious days. Because there are only a few such days per month, and because Ha Dzongda's brother needs to travel by bus from Tongsa to Thimphu, getting it all together takes time.

This is the big day. Ha Dzongda's brother in is town, and today's date is auspicious. Six monks arrive at the house in the early morning. They chant prayers and make *tormas* (offerings made from butter and dough), waiting for the people and Ha Dzongda's brother to arrive.

Today's audience comprises about 15 people, most of whom are relatives of Ha Dzongda's brother. About six of them live in the house; the remaining kinfolk have their own issues to address, once the *lu* has been dealt with. I am also in the audience; I feel my main tasks are to make myself invisible and to remember what I have seen.

Ha Dzongda's brother and his relatives practice in the Nyingma tradition (the smaller of the two Buddhist orders in Bhutan). Today, three Nyingma deities will visit us through the brother's body: Damchen, Drangsong, and Tsumara. Ha Dzongda's brother is dressed in an embroidered robe and will wear three hats in succession, one for each of the deities. A throne for the brother has been set up in a corner of the room.

Each deity will have an important and distinct role. Damchen is a senior but relatively remote presence. He will provide, through the brother's mouth, general directions and tonality for today's spirit encounter. Damchen is generally known for taking care of high lamas and assisting in the identification of children who are reincarnates of former lamas.

Drangsong is the overall head of *lu* spirits. He is crucial for today's encounter because he will give a concrete framework for subduing the *lu* living under this house and plaguing family members. The spirit hero today will be Tsumara. He will stay with us longer and take the exact steps to chase away the *lu*. If there is time, and if Ha Dzongda's brother still has enough energy, Tsumara will also deal with the problems of the other members of the audience.

Ha Dzongda's brother sits on the floor in the center of the room. The monks continue to chant their prayers. Every so often, they pick up their instruments and make the piercing, cacophonous sounds of Buddhist ritual. Everyone seems a little on edge to me. Ha Dzongda's brother cannot simply demand that the deities appear. Everyone must work hard in a cooperative enterprise; even then, they will need the good circumstances of an auspicious day.

At the beginning, the brother sits quietly, unobtrusively. Then, a storm begins to gather force. Ha Dzongda's brother breathes faster and faster.

His eyes roll back; soon we can see only the whites, as if he had been born blind. The brother leaps to his feet and begins to dance and whirl around the room, his body distorted in stiff, unworldly dimensions. The drums beat faster and faster as they keep time with the air whooshing in and out of the brother's lungs.

Damchen has entered the brother's body! Damchen begins to speak through the brother's mouth, in a cascade of words that no one in the room can understand. The people call out to Damchen: Stop! Please! Say something in the language of humans!

And so Damchen begins to speak in formal Tibetan. It is a language that Ha Dzongda's brother has never studied or spoken, but the words pour out. A woman who speaks Tibetan stands and follows the brother as he leaps around the room in his mad dance, translating the best she can.

When Damchen is finished addressing the audience and monks, Ha Dzongda's brother gathers his strength and takes a tremendous leap. To our eyes, he has flown across the room. The brother lands squarely on top of the throne. Several people jump to their feet and rush over to the brother, to help him change into Drangsong's hat.

Drangsong's dance is much like Damchen's, except that the brother's breathing and dancing become more frenetic. The brother whirls over to the monks and assaults them with criticism of their prayer and ritual. The monks, even while they are chanting, look chastened and frightened.

I sit in my corner struggling, as usual, with the right and left halves of my brain. The left side asks Why this, why that? The right side tries to subdue the left and to let the event happen on its own terms.

Another leap and the brother lands again on the throne. Drangsong's hat is replaced by Tsumara's. Ha Dzongda's brother is ready to get down to business with the *lu.*

By now, Ha Dzongda's brother is puffing like the Little Engine That Could. No ordinary person could tolerate such a rush of oxygen, but the brother becomes more intense, more animated as the minutes go by.

Ha Dzongda's brother whirls out of the room, and the audience follows. He traverses a hallway and ends up in a little storeroom in the corner of the house. A friend explains to me that it is the realm of the *lu!* And there, before a wide-eyed group of family members, Ha Dzongda's brother subdues the *lu* with a torrent of Tibetan words and dancing.

When the brother is finished with the *lu,* he dances back to the main room and signals his intention to deal with the issues of individual family members. First he deals with an unusual task. Ha Dzongda's brother dances over to the corner in which I have concealed myself, for a face-to-face encounter. My heart sinks. Have I offended Ha Dzongda's brother? Am I about to receive the same excoriation delivered to the monks just minutes before?

The translator struggles to keep up with Ha Dzongda's words. Look to the goddess Tara, says the brother to me. Let Tara be your guide and inspiration. (Later, I return home with a scroll painting of Tara, and she in reality becomes an inspiration.)

The brother turns to other members of the audience, counseling them. And then, in an instant, a profound exhaustion overcomes him. He staggers over to throne and begins the journey back to ordinary human existence. It is over.

Now, whenever I visit Tongsa or think about important moments in Bhutan, memories of Ha Dzongda's brother come back. In so many ways, he represents the magic of this place. A humble, unimportant man controls a life-restoring ritual and chastises the professionals, thus turning institutional religion on its head. He speaks for the most powerful local deities, strengthening and articulating Bhutan's bond with religious traditions that reach across the millennia. He cures illness, reestablishes self-confidence and inner peace, and in my case, creates a bond with the goddess Tara.

What Do Monks Do?

Sometimes we close our eyes and imagine the colors of Bhutan. Green emerges, because this is a land of luxuriant, endless forests. Blues are in our minds too, as we recall the crystalline skies of alpine mountains. But if we stay with this exercise a little longer, red seems like the main thing. The red of silk *kiras* worn by handsome women. Red bands on temple walls. Above all, the red of monks' robes.

In Bhutan, you encounter monks at every turn. They join the crowds in markets, sit patiently on the sidelines of archery matches, roam narrow trails on the sides of ridges, stuff themselves into Toyota Land Cruisers, and, in the case of the highest monks of all, sit alongside the king in photographs hanging on walls.

You might begin to wonder what monks do. Part of the answer is obvious and seems to be analogous to Catholic monastic communities in the West. Many Bhutanese monks live in monasteries, say their prayers, participate in group ceremonies, and provide manual labor and skilled services for the monk community. The rest of the answer is much more interesting.

First, the basics. As we mentioned in the introduction, the Buddhism found in Bhutan is technically a branch of Tibetan Buddhism. Thus virtually all of the observations made in this book about Buddhist practices in Bhutan would apply to traditional Tibetan culture as well. We frequently use the term "Tantric Buddhism" to refer to the Buddhism of both countries.

In Bhutan, some monks are paid by the government, while others are supported solely by private donations. The subsidized monks are members of the Kagyu order, which is the official state religion of Bhutan. (The full name of this order is Drukpa Kagyu, but in this sketch we shortened it to Kagyu.)

The Kagyu state religion is intricately organized. The chief executive monk is called the Je Khenpo. Under him are four monks who are, respectively, the masters of religious teachings, literary teachings, songs and liturgy, and philosophy. Under them are a staircase of monk leaders who provide the structure of a centralized form of governance. All in all, the model might look familiar if you have been a member of a large, institutional denomination of Christianity.

The rest of Bhutan's monks are members of the Nyingma order. Their organizational structure is indistinct and fluid. The Nyingma tradition includes a blend of lifestyles, belief systems, and lines of command that seem unique, as if "Made in the Himalayas" were stamped on them. Nyingma monks survive by the generosity of their donors.

Most monks in Bhutan are men, but there are handful of nuns called *anims*. Tantric Buddhism sends confusing messages about women. For example, nuns are always under the supervision of male monks and seem to be confined to minor religious roles. On the other hand, female goddesses and spirits are frequently powerful, inspiring, or terrifying, depending on which one you have in mind.

Up to now, we have been using the all-encompassing term "monk." It turns out that religious leaders in Tantric Buddhism come in different forms. The governance of this religion turns out to be elaborate and often different from Western preconceptions.

These are the words one should know:

Gelong—ordained monks who live in *dzongs* or *gompas*.

Rinpoche—a title meaning "great precious one." It is an honorific term for certain *tulkus* (see the next definition).

Tulku—a person who is a reincarnation of a deceased great master. A *tulku* may be a *gelong* or may live in the community as a married person. He may be an elevated religious leader or may be an ordinary person. Once a *tulku*, always a *tulku*.

Gomchen—lay monks who straddle the line between the monastic community and ordinary village life. Most of them are members of the Nyingma order. They are numerous and essential to the life of isolated communities, where they stand in for ordained monks.

Lama—a term widely misunderstood in the West. "Lama" and "monk" are not synonyms. Lamas may be ordained monks, or they may be laypeople with extraordinary religious gifts. They might be celibate, or they may have multiple wives, a thriving family, and a secular job. In any event, they are supposed to be religious leaders, no matter what lifestyle they may occupy.

Now, to the core question. Clearly, the government and people of Bhutan have made a major investment in *gelong, rinpoches, tulkus, gomchen,* and lamas. In turn, what do they do for their sponsors?

These men (and a few women) deliver a range of spiritual services that may startle the Western mind. Their competencies span the territory between earthy and elemental to unspeakably abstract, and everything in between.

The one thing that Buddhist professionals do not do is social service (at least, not in the Western sense). Westerners are accustomed to ministers, priests, and rabbis who operate community schools, run hospitals, and organize international relief initiatives. That kind of social service does not exist in Tantric Buddhism. But the things that Buddhist professionals do within the religious realm are boggling.

We are especially struck by the blend of the old and the new. Tantric Buddhist practice is a complex and diverse mixture of the old religion, based on local deities, and formal Buddhism (which was introduced to the region in the 8th century). Buddhist religious professionals administer rituals across the board.

Another example of what monks do lies in the difference between the popular and the abstract. Popular Buddhism is a belief system full of rules, rewards, and punishments. If you follow the rules and accumulate merit, your next life will be a pleasant one. If you break the rules, you may be reborn as a rabid dog. Abstract Buddhism, on the other hand, is centered on personal enlightenment. Its concepts of emptiness, nonself, and meditational visualization have practically nothing to do with the "if-then" logic of popular Buddhism.

Somehow, Buddhist professionals are supposed to operate at both the popular and abstract levels. As a practical matter, most of them cannot and end up functioning 90 percent at the popular level and 10 percent at the abstract. But the best lama is comfortable with both.

For another example of the range of monkly tasks, please consider the tools of the Buddhist trade. Even the first-time visitor to Bhutan will see monks doing unexpected things. For example, monks dance, paint art on the walls of temples, play music on human thighbones, and spend the entire night sitting on stone floors, chanting prayers. In addition, Buddhist professionals are expected to know whether a proposed action is auspicious or not. They unearth the answer through a process known as divination.

And just how does divination occur? In the most basic sense, Buddhist professionals look for omens—things that happen in daily life that suggest either risk or good fortune. An example could be an attempt to build a *chorten*. During the second day of work, one of the workmen cuts a tree to use as the *chorten*'s central pillar. But the tree is the wrong kind, is crooked, and hurts the worker's back when it is carried to the site. Three bad omens in a row, and the project is abandoned.

Sometimes, divination happens by rolling dice or counting beads on a rosary. A number of lamas are famous for their ability to find auspicious signs by looking in a mirror. Other lamas can divine auspicious signs with no tools at all.

In fact, a few Buddhist professionals become so adept at divination that it is their-full time job. We call them "oracles," or "oracle priests." Oracles are famous for their roles in the history of Tibet, and to this day the Dalai Lama consults the State Oracle, who lives in Dharamsala, India.

But the most pervasive tool of divination is astrology. In Western culture, astrology is serious business for some and a subject of derision for others. In any event, it is not usually an important part of Western religions. In Bhutan, however, astrology is a fundamental element of life, both civil and religious.

A few laymen are competent in astrology, but it is mainly within the jurisdiction of religious professionals. The influence of lama/astrologers spreads across the country in countless ways. Do you want good luck in tomorrow's archery tournament? Consult the astrologer. Should you start your new business on the first day of the month? Talk it over with the astrologer.

Astrologers even decide when the year starts. The Bhutanese calendar is expected to start each year within a several-week slot in the spring.

However, only a senior astrologer knows the exact day on which the year will commence. The country waits in suspense, unable to plan religious festivals and other events that need to be coordinated with the auspicious days within the calendar. Finally, the astrologer announces when the year will begin, and planning can take place.

If we used elapsed hours as the measuring stick for monk services, then surrogate praying will probably come out on top. Bhutanese rely on the professionals to say prayers for the people and their families. Laypeople can say prayers to a certain extent, and many of them fervently pray every morning. But serious, sustained prayers cannot be said by the people themselves. Only the professionals know the requisite language and ritual.

The situation is similar to Roman Catholicism during the days in which prayers needed to be said in Latin. However, there is a difference. In traditional Roman Catholicism, a priest (or perhaps two priests) said prayers for an hour or so. In Tantric Buddhism, a team of monks and lamas (typically six to eight) says prayers all day long, and sometimes the entire night as well.

There is one human event that causes the monk teams to intensify their service, multiplying their surrogate praying by orders of magnitude. It is not birth, or marriage, or some lifetime rite of Buddhist passage. It is death.

Because death is the point at which the process of reincarnation begins, it is fundamentally important to the people of Bhutan. For 49 days after this life ends, family members, monks, and lamas engage in complex and expensive rituals to help the decedent achieve a beneficial reincarnation. This is not a time for local deities or any of the other elements of folk religion. Instead, the services of the monks and lamas are essential. The professionals of formal Buddhism go to work with an unmatched intensity.

Western people sometimes have mixed feelings about Buddhist religious professionals. We are accustomed to praying for ourselves, and surrogate prayer might strike us as an institutional mechanism of control. We might be surprised by the degree to which Bhutanese families impoverish themselves with the cost of death rituals. We might find it easier to relate to the Nyingma tradition, with its empowering of laypeople, than the more hierarchal orders of Buddhism. We might wish that women had a more clear position of equality. Some of us would be uneasy with divination.

On the other hand, many of us sense that the Bhutanese have something we want but will never have. No matter how many pop psych movements arise in our culture, we will probably never have the feeling of cultural and religious unity that Bhutanese take for granted. Lacking the steady guideposts of Buddhist teaching, many of us will live a me-centered life, not seeing that each us of is an infinitesimal grain of sand. And without the constant reminder of reincarnation, many of us will be greedy stewards of the natural world, leaving behind a planet we have diminished.

GURU RINPOCHE

Guru Rinpoche is the most important Buddhist saint in Bhutan. His wisdom and
heroism provide daily inspiration to a large part of the Bhutanese population.

Treasure Seekers

In the preceding sketches, we have met quite a cast of characters. There is, of course, the monumental figure of Guru Rinpoche, whose energy, wisdom, and miraculous powers define the heart of Bhutan. Many Bhutanese would say that the Shabdrung would be number two on the list. Without him, Bhutan might not have emerged as a political entity. The Bhutanese would also include their four remarkable kings high in the rankings.

This sketch brings forth two additional human characters and a new concept. The humans are Pema Lingpa and Khyentse Rinpoche. The concept is treasure seeking.

We will start with treasure seeking. It might take you a little while to grasp the thinking here, because we Westerners do not have anything like it. In a nutshell, treasures, in the Tantric Buddhist tradition, are religious texts and artifacts that are hidden by great lamas during their lifetimes. These things are called *terma*. Years after the lamas' deaths, various people find the treasures and reveal them to their contemporaries. The finders are called *terton*.

In effect, the tradition of *terma* and *terton* is one of several routes by which Buddhist religious teaching is passed down to future generations. The other routes are the usual ones—oral tradition, told around campfires and in smoky kitchens, and formal written teachings, stored in monasteries and libraries.

The confusing thing about *terma* is that they take such different forms. Sometimes, *terma* are literally texts written on paper, hidden in the crack of a rock or in the back of a cave. Other times, the word "*terma*" is used to indicate sacred objects that are found by a *terton,* but which are not texts in their own right. In yet other cases, *terma* never exist physically. Instead, the teachings we call *terma* are directly intuited by a *terton* during a vision.

But once you get past the newness of it all, you see that treasure seeking has had a remarkably beneficial effect on certain orders of Tantric

Buddhism. The *terma* tradition accommodates evolution. By attributing *terma* to old masters, society gives the teaching immediate credibility. But by having a flexible attitude toward the identity of the *terton* and the content of the *terma*, society opens itself up to a flood of new thinking. Indeed, the Nyingma order of Buddhism, one of the two important orders in Bhutan, is almost entirely based on *terma* originally hidden by Guru Rinpoche and subsequently discovered by a number of *terton*.

Contrast that to religious traditions based solely on formal documentation. One might say that they are in ever-present danger of becoming rigid and intolerant. In their zeal to follow ancient texts literally, the practitioners and their tradition might lose the capacity to mold themselves to new times and changed human needs. There are those who say that the Geluk order of Tibetan Buddhism, a politically powerful order to which the Dalai Lama belongs, suffered exactly that fate during much of its history.

Given the importance of treasure finding in the Tantric Buddhist tradition, one would think that *terton* were, by and large, high-ranking religious professionals. Not so. Few of them were monks. Many of them were, in reality, unconventional free spirits who flew in the face of prevailing behavior and morality. We will have much more to say about these remarkable, off-the-wall people in the sketch "Kunley, Where Are You When We Need You?"

The most famous *terton* in premodern Bhutan was a charismatic and controversial fellow called Pema Lingpa (16th century). During his lifetime, he established three monasteries in the central part of Bhutan and created many sacred dances, which came to him in visions. He was best known for discovering *terma*—ultimately Pema Lingpa became a well-known *terton* throughout the Tibetan Cultural Area. To this day, the descendants of Pema Lingpa claim a high rung in the social hierarchy of Bhutan.

The curious Western mind wants to know the details of treasure finding. What do *terma* look like? How do *terton* know where to find them? How do we know that *terma* are authentic, or that *terton* are trustworthy people?

We have never discovered clear answers to those questions. But the following passages at least give hints about the professional life of a *terton*.

They describe Pema Lingpa at the very beginning of his career and illustrate two important points about *terma*: treasures can be actual written texts of religious teachings, or symbolic objects.

> He had a series of dreams, trances and visions, culminating in the discovery of his first *terma*, a chest containing a text…in a rock by a river. He transcribed this into Tibetan and, after a series of visions, which gave him further instructions, bestowed the initiation for the public.
>
> His next treasure was discovered in the same place shortly afterwards. A large crowd was in attendance….As on the previous occasion, he dived naked into the river to find the entrance to the rock, this time bearing a lighted butter lamp. He extracted an image of the Buddha and a sealed skull with miraculous substances.[6]

Initially, our feeling about treasure finding was probably typical of many Western people—respect for the Bhutanese who believe in *terma* and *terton,* but a nagging sense that treasure finding is a tradition that cannot survive in the modern world. Then, as we became more familiar with the life of a great 20th-century lama named Khyentse Rinpoche, our feeling changed. This man, who died in 1991, was, in addition to many other things, a *terton.* He discovered treasures by direct intuition and transmitted them to students around the world through teaching and writing.

Khyentse Rinpoche's writings turned us around. *Terma* no longer seemed like historical curiosities. Instead, they had a stirring and immediate connection to our own lives.

The original author of Khyentse Rinpoche's *terma* is believed to be Guru Rinpoche, who created them in the 8th century. We have read many other English translations of *terma* attributed to Guru Rinpoche and have frequently found them to be rough going. Khyentse Rinpoche's *terma* are different. They are poetic, wise, and entirely accessible to the Western mind.

Khyentse Rinpoche was born in 1910 in Eastern Tibet. He left home at the age of 13, studied with lamas, and then went into 13 years of silent retreat in remote hermitages and caves. Khyentse Rinpoche matured into a highly respected lama but was forced to flee Tibet during the Chinese takeover in the 1950s.

Khyentse Rinpoche spent much the remainder of his life in Bhutan, although he traveled to Europe and the United States and even managed to return to Tibet three times later in his life. He sponsored the reconstruction of Samye Monastery (Tibet's first Buddhist monastery), a project supported in part by a large contribution from Bhutan's king. In 1991, failing health forced him to cancel a fourth trip to Tibet. Instead, he spent three months in retreat near the famous *lhakhang* called the Tiger's Lair in Western Bhutan, and then died peacefully. His cremation was a three-day ceremony that included a crowd of 50,000 people, the largest gathering in Bhutan's history.

The life and teaching of Khyentse Rinpoche are presented in a magnificent book called *Journey to Enlightenment* by Matthieu Ricard. In our opinion, this book is itself a treasure. We know of no better way to get a sense of the sweep of Himalayan high country or the substance of a spiritual leader who was the real thing.

Please put yourself in a contemplative frame of mind and savor the writing of Khyentse Rinpoche. Treasures indeed (which came to Khyentse Rinpoche by direct intuition).

On water and ice

> In the heart of winter, the chill freezes lakes and rivers; water becomes so solid that it can bear men, beasts, and carts. As spring approaches, earth and water warm up and thaw. What then remains of the hardness of ice: Water is soft and fluid, ice hard and sharp, so we cannot say they are identical; but neither can we say that they are different, because ice is only solidified water, and water is only melted ice.
>
> The same applies to our perception of the world around us. To be attached to the reality of phenomena, to be tormented by attraction and repulsion, by pleasure and pain, gain and loss, fame and obscurity, praise and blame, creates a solidity in the mind. What we have to do, there-

fore, is melt the ice of concepts into the living water of the freedom within.[7]

Sunlight on a crystal

When sunlight falls on a crystal, lights of all colors of the rainbow appear; yet they have no substance that you can grasp. Likewise, all thoughts in their infinite variety— devotion, compassion, harmfulness, desire—are utterly without substance. This is the mind of the Buddha. There is no thought that is something other than voidness; if you recognize the void nature of thoughts at the very moment they arise, they will dissolve. Attachment and hatred will never be able to disturb the mind. Deluded emotions will collapse by themselves. No negative actions will be accumulated, so no suffering will follow.[8]

Compassion

The great teachers of the past considered the most precious teaching to be the inseparability of voidness and compassion. They cultivated love, compassion, joy and equanimity—the four limitless thoughts out of which the ability to help others arises effortlessly. Motivated by compassion for all beings, we should establish firmly in our hearts the intention to attain enlightenment for the sake of others. Without this intention, our compassion will be a pale imitation of the real things. It is said, "To wish happiness for others, even for those who want to do us great harm, is the source of consummate happiness." When finally we reach this level, compassion for all beings arises by itself in a way that is utterly uncontrived.[9]

Meditation and realization

Realization occurs in three stages: understanding, experiences, and true realization. The first is theoretical understanding and comes from studying the teachings. It is necessary, of course, but it is not very stable. It is like a patch, sewn on a cloth, which will eventually come off. Theoretical understanding is not strong enough to weather the good and bad things that happen to you in life. If difficulties arise, no theoretical understanding will allow you to overcome them.

As for experiences in meditation, they are, like mist, bound to fade away. If you concentrate on your practice in a secluded place, you are sure to have various experiences. But such experiences are very unreliable, and it is said, "Meditators who run after their experiences, like a child running after a beautiful rainbow, will be misled." When you practice intensely, you may have flashes of clairvoyance and various signs of accomplishments, but all they do is to foster expectations and pride—they are just devilish tricks and the source of obstacles....

But someone with true realization is like a mighty mountain that cannot be shaken by any wind, or like the unchanging blue sky. Good or adverse circumstances, even in their thousands, will provoke no attachment or aversion, no expectation or doubt at all....For such a person, all deluded perceptions are exhausted. The result is that all circumstances, whether adverse or favorable, will further his progress on the path.[10]

TEACHING THE TULKU "HIGH FIVE"

It is a sunny, peaceful afternoon in the capital city of Thimphu. We are visiting our friends Sonam Jatso and Tshering Yangzom, and the usual family things are happening. Grandmas, sisters, aunts, and assorted friends rush in and out of the room, bringing tea, cracked corn, and the other honorific foods of Bhutan. The faces of the current king, the second king, and the third king look down on us from their photographs on the walls. Sweethearted mother-in-law gives us a big smile, with all the bright-red innocence of a confirmed chewer of betel nut.

The main event is the children, as it is the world around. A five-year-old boy, named Lhaksam, and his three-year-old sister Dorji Tso, have instantly uncovered the way to communicate with English-speaking visitors. How is it that human beings with so little time on this earth can be so clever? Of course, these children are growing up in a house where five languages are regularly spoken, so they are developing some language wiring in their brains that we will never have.

Dorji Tso is dressed in Western clothing, which is the normal way "urban" Bhutanese now dress at home. However, Lhaksam is dressed in red and gold, the colors of a high-ranking lama. This cute little boy is a *tulku,* a reincarnation of a prominent lama who lived years ago in Tibet.

Our son, Drew, is with us. He has come on this trip to help set up one of Bhutan's first Internet cafes. Every day here has yielded uncommon experiences. This afternoon, for example, is the first time Drew has made friends with a five-year-old person who is actually a high-ranking religious eminence, reborn from a life on the Tibetan plateau.

Drew has a natural aptitude with children. After the first 30 minutes of introductory interaction, Drew is playing games with them. He decides to teach Lhaksam the "high five."

Give me five! Squeals of laughter. On the side! More of the untouched delight in which children specialize. Down low!

Drew suckers him. Lhaksam winds up for a major downward traveling five, and Drew withdraws his hand at the last minute. Whoosh. Lhaksam looks startled, and then, with a face-wide grin, gets the joke. Down low, Drew says again, and this time there is a solid whack. All right!

When Lhaksam was first identified as a *tulku* at the age of four, his parents' lives changed. Now, he is no longer just a little boy. Lhaksam needs to be fed special foods, dressed in the colors of a lama, and spiritually nurtured. A bed has been set up for him in the family's altar room. The family's attitude toward him changed in many subtle ways. Even little Dorji Tso gets the idea. When she is mad or impatient with him, he is still Lhaksam. But when she wants to butter him up, she calls him *tulku*.

The family will lose Lhaksam in several years. He will become a member of a large monastery in southern India, where he will begin the arduous journey of Buddhist monastic training. We sense a bittersweet feeling in his parents. Sorrow for the loss of his company, but pride that the family has contributed to the Nyingma tradition at such a high level, and confidence that Lhaksam will grow into a wise and caring person.

There is another positive point about having a monk or lama in the family. In Bhutan, death is the single most important religious event. Most Buddhists are very concerned about a successful transition to their next life, and they believe that the crossing cannot be made without elaborate help from the professionals and adherence to complex ritual. All of this is expensive and, typically, the heaviest financial burden a family will face. However, a monk or lama in the family can make a big difference, both by lowering the cost and by providing intensity and quality in the religious experience.

The process by which *tulkus* are discovered is well established. Important lamas are expected to predict their own rebirths before they die. The predictions include some information about the location of the new *tulku* and the nature of his family. Two or three years after a lama's death, officials of his monastery launch the search, armed both with his predictions and hints provided by their own visions. A candidate child is supposed to give certain signs, including knowledge about the deceased lama's life. Discovery is a widespread occurrence; there are thousands of *tulkus* these days, throughout the Tibetan Cultural Area and in communities of Tantric Buddhists across the world.

The *tulku* tradition got its start centuries ago in Tibet. Although it was initially confined to the Karma Kagyu school, it rapidly spread to the

Paro Valley in spring. Paro Dzong is in the foreground, while the ancient watch-tower (now the National Museum) is visible on the hill.

Lush terraces in a low-altitude area of Eastern Bhutan.

Yaks in a field of dwarf bamboo near Gantey Valley, Central Bhutan .

Farmhouse near Bumthang, in Central Bhutan. See the sketch "Riddles Lie Here."

[Above] Temple for a local deity named Garub Wangchuck in Eastern Bhutan. Many large rocks and cliffs are associated with local deities. See the sketch "Caring for the Earth."

[Right] This tiny temple is dedicated to a female water deity, known as a *lu*. There are a huge number of such temples throughout Bhutan. See the sketch "The Spirits Within."

The Tongsa Dzong, in Central Bhutan, dominates the countryside from a commanding position. See the sketch "Riddles Lie Here."

Chendebji Chorten, in Central Bhutan, is in the Nepalese style, with eyes painted on the four walls of the upper spire. A *mani* wall tells the story of the *chorten*.

Meditation huts in Western Bhutan. Devout Buddhists sometimes spend three years, three months, three weeks, and three days in such places.

A scene from the interior of the famous temple Taktsang Lhakhang (Tiger's Lair) in Western Bhutan.

An archery tournament at Tongsa Dzong, Central Bhutan, celebrating the king's birthday. See the sketch "An Enterprise of Polarities."

Wah ha! Team members dancing and singing, celebrating a hit in Western Bhutan.

The governor of Ha, Western Bhutan, showing how it is done (in spite of the teases from the dancing girls).

The Archery Chorten near Thimphu, Western Bhutan. The insert shows the archery goddess, who dwells within the *chorten*. See the sketch "An Enterprise of Polarities."

Co-author Russ Carpenter attempting to hit that tiny target, 460 feet away (in Thimphu, Western Bhutan). See the sketch "Learning the Ropes."

Booby prize in Ha, Western Bhutan. If you were unable to hit the target by noon, you had to wear one of these.

Harvest time in Ugyencholing, Central Bhutan.

Eager spectators in Central Bhutan.

Two lovely persons celebrating the king's birthday in Tongsa, Central Bhutan.

Another proof that the Bhutanese may be the world's most handsome people (near Bumthang, Central Bhutan).

[Above] Silk weaver in Eastern Bhutan.

[Right] Weaving *yathra* near Bumthang, Central Bhutan.

Burning juniper in the early morning (Eastern Bhutan). A scene repeated in all parts of Bhutan.

The Thimphu Tsechu (festival), Western Bhutan.

Lhaksam being confirmed as a *tulku* in the Nyingma monastery in Mysore, India.

The co-authors' son Drew Carpenter a giving lesson, at home in Thimphu, Western Bhutan. See the sketch "Teaching the Tulku 'High Five.'"

Lamas leading a prayer ceremony in Eastern Bhutan.

Most families in Bhutan reserve their best room as a shrine room. This is an example of a family's altar in Western Bhutan.

A door leading to the temple of the local deities, Eastern Bhutan.

Prayer wheels within the exterior wall of a temple in Thimphu, Western Bhutan.

Prayer flags are everywhere in Bhutan. These are at a high mountain pass in Central Bhutan.

Two young monks in Thimphu, Western Bhutan.

Damchen, an important local deity. He takes care of high lamas and assists in the identification of *tulkus* (reincarnated lamas).

Drangsong, another important local deity, is the head of the *lu* spirits (aquatic female deities). See the sketch "Ha Dzongda's Brother."

This striking creature is a *lu*. See the sketch "The Spirits Within."

A local deity from Tongsa, Central Bhutan.

Violence is a cornerstone of Tantric Buddhist art. Most of the explanations are abstractly philosophical—for example, the subduing of unskilled patterns of thinking. See the sketch "Sacred Paint."

Painting *thangkas* in Thimphu, Western Bhutan.

The master painter, Lopen Gyem Dorji, at work in Thimphu, Western Bhutan.

Sexual meditation is an essential element of Tibetan Buddhism. The paintings showing this meditation in practice are called *yab-yum*. They occur in two styles: fierce (see the example above) and peaceful (see the examples below).

The erect penis is a common motif throughout the Bhutanese countryside. Many explanations are heard. Perhaps the most common is that they scare away evil spirits. See the sketches "Is Sex Necessary?" and "Sacred Paint."

A beautiful and sophisticated example of *yab-yum* art, in carved slate, Western Bhutan.

Perhaps the most common theme in the folk art of Bhutan. The Four Friends cooperate to produce a bountiful fruit tree.

The Wheel of Life. An intricate, powerful, graphic portrayal of Tantric Buddhist concepts. See the sketch "A World of Circles."

other orders. It is easy to see why. When you think about the succession problems faced by organizations of men who do not have children, you realize that belief in *tulkus* is a problem solver.

Leaders could have been recruited from a lama's extended family, but the *tulku* tradition sidestepped the danger of running out of candidates within the family. Furthermore, child *tulkus* could be discovered from a variety of human gene pools over the generations, thus avoiding inbreeding. Children could be trained for leadership from a young age. They would immediately benefit from the authority of their predecessors, without spending the first half of their lives climbing political ladders.

The Dalai Lama himself is a *tulku,* and many Westerners have learned about the process of *tulku* discovery from movies about the Dalai Lama's early life. However, those movies, as well as most of the other popular images of Tibet, have given us a dramatically incorrect and idealized view of Tibetan culture during the time of the Dalai Lama's 13 predecessors. The current Dalai Lama seems to be the most reasonable, calm, and humane of men. Western people tend to extrapolate his qualities, leaping to the conclusion that Tibetan culture throughout its history has consistently shared those qualities.

One could say that the story of the Dalai Lamas began in the 14th century with the establishment of a new order of Buddhism in Tibet called the Geluks. A remarkable scholar by the name of Tsongkhapa developed a synthesis of Tibetan Buddhist practices and doctrines. Tsongkhapa's system received widespread approval and became the doctrinal basis of the Geluk order, to which all 14 Dalai Lama's have belonged.

The third head of the Geluks, Sonam Gyatsho, was another key person in the history of the order. He was caught in a power struggle between the Geluks (referred to as the "Yellow Hats") and the Kagyus (referred to the "Red Hats"). In an effort to strengthen his position, he made an alliance with the Mongolians, converting Altan Khan to Tantric Buddhism. The title "Dalai Lama" was actually crafted by the Khan, who applied it to Sonam Gyatsho and his two predecessors.

The fourth Dalai Lama was not even Tibetan—he was the Khan's great-grandson. That was either a shrewd political move or a lucky religious occurrence, depending on your point of view.

By the time of the fifth Dalai Lama, conflict between the Yellow Hats and Red Hats was intense, with the Dalai Lama's enemies, the Red Hats, gaining strength. So the Dalai Lama called in military troops from his old friends, the Mongolians, who literally crushed the opposition. An important Red Hat king was executed, and Red Hat practitioners fled to outlying regions of Tibet, Sikkim, and Bhutan.

A new idea then emerged. Tibetans came to believe that the fifth Dalai Lama, in addition to being the Ocean of Wisdom Teacher (the literal translation of Dalai Lama), was an "emanation" of one of the most important Tantric deities. At this point, the Dalai Lama became the overall ruler of Tibet. Thus in the space of a single lifetime, the fifth Dalai Lama had evolved astonishingly. He began as the leader of a order that seemed to be losing ground. He ended as the ruler of a order with a monopoly on religious power, as the chief of state, and as a quasi god.

There is more. The Manchus took power in China, and shortly thereafter the fifth Dalai Lama made a deal with them as well. In exchange for their willingness to use Chinese power to protect the Yellow Hats, the fifth Dalai Lama agreed to establish a special priest/patron relationship with the Manchus. The fifth Dalai Lama then constructed an immense mandala/palace in Lhasa and named it the Potala.

The sixth through thirteenth Dalai Lamas were, by and large, less imposing figures. A number of them had short lives, perhaps murdered by their opponents. Others were deposed and exiled. Political maneuvering was often left to the senior officials.

By making deals with the Mongolians and then the Chinese, the Geluks were playing a dangerous game. Foreign soldiers kept the Yellow Hats in power, but for centuries the Tibetans needed all their wits to keep their partners' power in check. They lost their gamble in 1951, when the Chinese took control of Tibet. Reprehensible, yes. But in light of the long history between the *tulkus* and China, perhaps not surprising.

In traditional Tantric Buddhism, *tulku* status was the source of both prestige and power. Having a *tulku* in the family, especially if he were the reincarnate of a high lama, made a big difference to a family's wealth and social standing. It was, of course, a situation tailor-made for occasional manipulation and maneuvering.

Here is a fragment of a street song from Lhasa that illustrates the point. It makes fun of a pretentious, highborn woman who was scheming to have her son declared the next Dalai Lama. She was burning incense under her dress to sanctify her genitals, thus preparing them for delivery of the next Ocean of Wisdom Teacher.

> The sun, which is the happiness of the world,
>
> has risen in Takpo.
>
> Her excellency, Mrs. Doring's
>
> ass, has become black with soot.[11]

One of the more remarkable stories of conflict over *tulkus* comes from Bhutan. You will recall learning about the Shabdrung earlier in this book. This monumental figure from the 17th century unified Bhutan, subduing daunting cultural and geographic obstacles. Toward the end of his life, the Shabdrung went on a spiritual retreat. He died during the retreat, although no one knows exactly when. For about 50 years, the tiny oligarchy ruling Bhutan kept his death a secret. They passed food through a trapdoor, forged written commands, and generally managed to trick the population into thinking that this towering presence, although still on retreat, was ruling the country.

Finally, in the early 18th century, the truth came out. For the next 40 years, rival factions argued over which of five different *tulku* candidates was the real thing. The dispute finally led to war. One of the rivals asked the Tibetan ruler to intervene, and Tibet then launched a full-scale invasion of Bhutan.

Ultimately, both China and Tibet sponsored peace negotiations. Meanwhile, some of the Bhutanese claimants died (some would say "conveniently"). The way was cleared to a settlement that might seem, in Western eyes, quite creative. The warring parties agreed that the Shabdrung had actually reincarnated in three different forms: "mind, body, and spirit." Each protagonist got a piece of the Shabdrung. Thereafter, there were *tulkus* of the *tulkus*, and the whole situation became comprehensible only to a serious student of Bhutanese history.

The story of *tulkus* can be rendered, like so many others in Bhutan, through multiple lenses. If you employ the skeptical Western lens, reincarnation of religious leaders might be seen as a convenient method of arranging succession at best, and an invitation for abuse at worst. Using the lens of the Bhutanese themselves, the tradition can be seen as the bedrock of a civilized society, passing down wisdom and experience from one generation to the next,

We have come to realize that there is a difference between thinking about Bhutanese culture in the abstract and experiencing it. That afternoon, while Drew was teaching Lhaksam the high five, we saw two wonderful things at once. There was the little boy whose pure delight in this new game gave good feelings to all of us. But we looked into his eyes and we saw a person who was kind and gentle beyond his years. The *tulku* will, beyond doubt, grow in extraordinary dimensions.

Tantra Demystified

This morning we tried an interesting experiment. We logged onto our favorite Internet search engine and typed in "Tantra." Up came 174,000 hits.

This little exercise suggested that the term "Tantra" and its derivatives have become an important part of our culture (or at least our Internet culture). But if you read some of the synopses in the search engine, your head will swim. The same thing will happen if you read books on Buddhism and Himalayan culture. What on earth does Tantra really mean?

We should not feel discouraged if we are flummoxed by this word. In 1971, a student of Buddhism, Herbert Guenther, called Tantrism "probably one of the haziest notions and misconceptions the Western mind has evolved."[12] If anything, the term has become even more baroque in the last decade, because in the minds of some people it now connotes a sleazy, countercultural attitude toward sex (which is also the reason why we had so many hits from our Internet search).

Herein we attempt a practical, brief clarification of Tantra and its derivations. Fortunately, once you strip away the baggage attached to Tantra and its cousins, they are perfectly reasonable and functional words.

Tantra is a Sanskrit word meaning warp or loom. By extension, it also means a work, or text, or handbook. *Tantric Buddhism, at the most simple level, is a school of Buddhism based on ancient texts, called Tantra, first written in India.*

Tantra were developed as part of an anti-establishment movement in India, reacting against the power of Buddhist universities and the increasingly rigid caste system. They were contrarian documents, challenging one social convention after another. The Tantra described doctrines and rituals for achieving enlightenment within a single lifetime. They were supposed to be kept secret and were thought to be so powerful that they could, in reality, be dangerous. Consequently, students of Tantra were required to practice under the supervision of a teacher, or guru.

Shortly after the time the Tantric movement in India gained strength (roughly the 7th century), Indian Buddhism overall began its slide into oblivion (a victim primarily of the Islamic invasion.) However, the Tantra were translated into Tibetan, and the Tantric Buddhist tradition migrated to the Himalayas, where it survives in Tibet, Bhutan, Mongolia, and other parts of the Himalayas and Central Asia.

From the beginning, separate collections of Tantra had evolved to serve different Indian cult groups. That tradition continues today, with each of the four major orders of Tantric Buddhism having its body of Tantric literature and ritual (although there is a considerable degree of overlap). Bhutan is probably the best place in the world to see the Tantric lifestyle in action.

Tantra are not organized in an orderly manner. They are the very opposite: messy and seemingly illogical. They celebrate what most religions repress: the human body, sexuality, violence, and death. Many of the insights unearthed by Freud, Jung, and their successors in the 19th and 20th centuries had already become the heart of Tantric practice in ancient India.

The core idea of Tantric Buddhism is this: if you want to achieve enlightenment in a single lifetime, you have to play with fire. You need to plunge deep into the psyche, unearth the issues lying in the repressed and dark corners, and make them the foundation of spiritual growth. You must make the body your cathedral.

Two things in the Tantric tradition stand out for Westerners—the astonishing use of visualization, and the emphasis on sexual meditation. Visualization happens within the individual, so the visitor to Bhutan will not see it in take place. But scenes of sexual meditation repeat themselves thousands of times in the art of Bhutan.

The sexual aspect is, of course, what makes the Tantra irresistible to the purveyors of Western popular culture. The Western world is now awash in psychobabble about the Tantric practices, most of which is so ignorant and childish that it is a pretty good laugh. The real thing is an astonishingly rigorous discipline requiring a lifetime to grasp.

We realize that we started too late. There are not enough years remaining in our lifetimes for us to do more than scratch the exterior of Tantric practice. But it is scratching of the most intriguing kind.

VAJRAPANI

Vajrapani (also called Chan Dorje) is a powerful Buddhist deity who is venerated throughout the Tibetan Cultural Area.

Sacred Paint

Visitors to Bhutan have a problem with their eyes and brains. There is so much flowing into the former and not enough capacity in the latter.

This smidgen of a country delivers a river of sensory perceptions. Consider, for example, these: the world's highest unclimbed mountain, perfectly preserved tropical jungles, tiny roads etched into the sides of cliffs, strangely resonant chanting in the early morning air, fortresses at the tops of mountain-goat ridges, water-driven prayer wheels in backcountry enclaves, silk dresses with intricate cascades of pattern and color, and the most handsome people you have ever seen. In all, more than most of us can absorb.

After you begin to parse your senses, you realize that there is an astonishment that stands above all others. It is made from walls and paint—simple things that, in their confluence, present a worldview and aesthetic sensibility that will stay with you for the rest of your life.

In this sketch we use the term "sacred paint" for the wall art of Bhutan. At the outset, we will make it clear that there are features of sacred paint that are beyond the grasp of most Western people. Two-dimensional Tantric art is often intended to serve as an object of a sophisticated form of meditation called visualization. We realize that we will never have these meditational powers and thus will never see the art in that realm. But the dimensions of sacred paint go far beyond meditation, and the riches that remain are plenty for us.

One issue with sacred paint is that there is so much of it. Two-dimensional art is literally everywhere: woven into clothing, on stone walls in remote corners of the Himalayas, on every wall of every house and store, surrounding the computers in the country's handful of Internet cafes, and from top to bottom of temples and monasteries.

You find yourself becoming inured to art. You realize that you need to look at sacred paint two square feet at a time. In larger doses, you are in danger of swamping your circuits.

When you slow down, marvels unfold. The art perfectly captures the paradox and fascination of this culture, in which erudition and shamanism exist side by side. On this wall, Buddhist archetypal figures remind us of some of the world's most elevated religious abstractions, such as duality, emptiness, and nonself. On that wall, true-to-life figures act out the earthy dramas of ambition, sexuality, retribution, serenity, and reconciliation.

On first encounter, some of the sacred paint seems formulaic. To Western eyes, important Tantric deities appear to have been produced from the same cookie cutters, with standardized colors, postures, and accoutrement. No matter where you are in Bhutan, Tibet, and nearby areas, a portrait of Vajrapani, for example, will look a lot like thousands of other portraits of Vajrapani. Gautama Buddha will be instantly recognizable, no matter who painted him, or when. In fact, art students are taught to paint the Buddha on a grid so that the proportions of his body will be the same everywhere.

Furthermore, portraits of the archetypal deities use artistic techniques we visitors might describe as primitive. The figures are always presented face out, precisely and uniformly frontal. There is no use of perspective. Even though many of the figures are portrayed in ostensibly wrathful poses, the portraits often seem static and remote. Visitors might be reminded of other archetypal portraiture they have seen, such as stone bas-relief portraits on the walls of Mayan or Egyptian temples.

Egypt is an especially interesting parallel. Sculptures and paintings of the big shots of ancient Egypt quickly seem repetitive and tedious. But if you spend a few days in the dusty back rooms of the Cairo Museum, absorbing the clay figures of ordinary people in their day-to-day lives, you see marvelous art, full of honest and engaging detail about life in ancient Egypt. In the same way, if you draw closer to sacred paint in Bhutan and look at the scenes surrounding the honorific portraits, the vitality and scope of the painting will be wondrous.

As your acquaintance with sacred paint deepens, you realize that there are two features of this art for which no other artistic experience has prepared you. Tantric painting is violent. And it is full of sexuality.

Your first hints about violence in sacred paint comes from the formal portraits we have already mentioned. Most Tantric deities are portrayed in two different forms—peaceful and wrathful. The peaceful forms are the very soul of serenity, compassion, and centeredness. They remind you of the Buddhist art of Southeast Asia (which is much more familiar to Western people than the Buddhist art of the Himalayas).

The very same deity who seems beatific in one portrait looks like a monster in the next. The Mona Lisa smiles are gone. These unpleasant characters—the wrathful forms—have dark bodies, piercing eyes, snarls, fangs, claws, helpless victims under clawed feet, and flames shooting out in all directions.

There is an official explanation for all this, which is that the deities must have a fierce side to deal with unhealthy thinking and malicious forces. That makes sense, given the overall Himalayan preoccupation with subduing the risks of spiritual and physical life. We may not be used to symbolism that is quite so strong, but the symbols' purposes are easy to grasp.

And the truth is that this form of sacred paint (the wrathful forms of important deities) is not really so frightening. As we have said, this is a highly stylized form of art. There is a certain rigidity and formalism in these wrathful forms that makes them seem abstract. They are not likely to wake you up in the middle of the night.

There is, however, more to the story. The eye-opening scenes of violence occur in the details. Look beyond the large-scale portraits to the scenes in the background.

If you get close to a wall of Tantric Buddhist painting, you encounter dismemberment, disembowelment, and impalement. Some figures drink blood from crushed skulls, while others pull intestines from living victims. Terrified prisoners sit on the ground awaiting their fates. Like the rest of the sacred paint in the background, this art is fluid, detailed, and convincing.

The same official explanation can be given for this art as well. That is, one can say that the violence just symbolizes the vigor with which unhealthy thinking must be rooted out and evil spirits contained. We are not so sure. This sacred paint stops us in our tracks. We are not willing to accept a simple explanation. To us, this art connects to ancient times, shamanistic religious traditions, and unsettling insights into the dark side of human nature. Maybe someday we will be willing to accept a packaged Buddhist explanation for this sacred paint, but we are not there yet. For now, we are attracted by the mystery and power of this art, which transcend verbal packaging.

The second feature relates to sex. We will have much more to say about the general role of sexuality in Bhutanese life in the sketch "Is Sex Necessary?" Here, we look at sex in art.

Many of us who were raised in the Western traditions are not prepared for sexuality in religious iconography. For example, most of us would be startled to see a painting of Jesus in sexual union, or of Abraham copulating with a female consort. But that is exactly the nature of much Tantric art. Buddhist deities of every level, from minor figures to the highest status, are frequently portrayed in sexual intercourse.

Sexual union is such a common theme in Tantric art that it has a name—*yab-yum*. It is highly stylized. Most of the time, intercourse is taking place in the sitting ("lotus") position. The male is facing the observer. The female is sitting in the male's lap, with her back toward the observer. If you see enough Tantric art, you encounter all of the erogenous zones, including breasts, nipples, erect penises, and vaginas. But overall, most *yab-yum* painting is fairly restrained and abstract.

When Western visitors first encountered Tantric art, many of them were scandalized. Here is an excerpt from Garnet Wolseley's 1860 book, *Narrative of the War with China*:

> Lust and sensuality is represented in its hideous nakedness and under its most disgusting aspect....The priests when exhibiting these beastly groups did so with the greatest apparent satisfaction, and seemed to gloat over the abominations before them, which to any but those of the most bestial dispositions must have been loathsome in the extreme. Surely it cannot be wondered at, that a people who thus deify lust, should be base and depraved, and incapable of any noble feelings or lofty aspirations after either the good or the great.[13]

But with the passage of time, the West has become accustomed to the spicy nature of sacred paint. In fact, Western writers now have a tendency to swoon over Tibetan art. Here is an example from Franco Maraini, a photographer who worked with a famous Tibetologist named Giuseppe Tucci:

> [The male/female pair is] the Absolute, the Ultimate, The First, the Eternal, the Everlasting, and the All-Pervading, in the form of a bejewelled prince voluptuously embracing his shakti. What fantastic imagination, what metaphysical daring, to represent the most abstract possible concept, a concept only definable by negatives, like mathematical infinity, by the most concrete, the most carnal picture that it is possible to imagine.[14]

Where, between these overheated extremes, does the truth lie? What is the sexuality in sacred paint about? Will we have a case, similar to that with wrathful deities, in which there is an official explanation that may or may not resemble what our native intelligence is telling us?

There is, indeed, an official explanation. *Yab-yum* paintings are said to symbolize the union of wisdom (the female figure) and compassion (the male figure). There are many other roles of sex in Tantric Buddhism, but in the realm of art, you will hear the official explanation from just about any Bhutanese you ask. And the same point of view has been encountered in just about every book we have read on Tantric art.

In fact, both Asian and Western commentators seem to suffer anxiety about this art. By and large, they seem determined to sanitize sacred paint. They might be driven to prove that sexual Tantric art is philosophical, abstract, and pristine and certainly not connected to the sensory realities of sex in ordinary life.

Some of the best examples of the official explanation occur in the writing of Robert Thurman, a professor from Columbia University (and an "ordained Buddhist layman"). Thurman might be the most widely known proponent of Tantric Buddhism in the Western world. He writes with inexhaustible passion and complete commitment to Buddhist principles. When he writes for a lay audience, he sets aside the usual scholarly understatements.

Here is Thurman on *yab-yum* painting. The material has been heavily condensed by us.

Yet if seen only at the "ordinary" level of physical union, the imagery...might seem to confirm so many of our long standing misperceptions of Tibetan Buddhism as a "primitive" mix of Buddhism and an indigenous animistic religion, as a corrupt and degenerate form of Buddhism, or as evidence of a culture in which rites and practices are based on, or even legitimize sexual extremes.

Nothing could be further from the truth. The father-mother union is a manifestation of the Buddha's highest spiritual essence, of enlightenment as the union of wisdom and compassion....

As modern depth psychology has come to recognize, images like this...represent the deepest archetypes of the unconscious, integrating the powerful, instinctual energies of life into a consciously sublimated and exalted state.

We can become [the female figure], burning with the unrestrained passion of love that experiences, indivisibly, individual satisfaction and the happiness of all beings. Being wisdom ourselves,...we see our compassion-consort as the absolute in action. We embrace him as if he were the universe itself, as if he were vast networks of galactic energies spread infinitely throughout the endless void, a creative darkness bursting with the brilliant light of power and beauty. And at the same time responding as [the male figure] we feel [the female figure] as the absolute at peace. We embrace wisdom as our true home, a calm so vast and free that it can be delicate and sensitive, the tender creative matrix. In union as wisdom and compassion, we are blissful in a sustained and sustaining way, radiating light streams of healing energy to all beings.[15]

Let us now take a deep breath and put our common sense to work. Does the foregoing word picture have a familiar ring to it? Without intending a shred of disrespect, we suggest that we have all been here before. We have encountered fellow human beings who, in their passion and zeal, sometimes fall into the trap of overselling.

Even if you had never been to any part of the Tibetan Cultural Area, you might suspect that the wisdom/compassion explanation may be just a bit too perfect. We have found that sex in Bhutan has both an abstract and down-to-earth aspect. Thurman presents a ringing explanation of the abstractions. But the practicalities of sex are just as attention getting. As we explain at greater length in "Is Sex Necessary?" sexual practices in Bhutan are as earthy and biological as anywhere else—perhaps more so.

Thus it is possible (and we would say probable) that sexuality in sacred paint is present for two reasons. One is that it in fact symbolizes an important part of Buddhist philosophy. The other is that it is a mirror of vigorous sexual practices going on in ordinary life.

For us, some of the most interesting insights about sacred paint have come from ordinary American citizens. For example, in Oregon we have done some "road shows," primarily trying to drum up interest in Bhutanese textiles, thus helping the weaving villages of Eastern Bhutan. We have experimented with a series of slides that are completely honest about the themes of sex and violence in Bhutanese art. We were concerned at first, but now realize how much both we and the audience have gained from these slides.

When we talk about sexual art, we dutifully report the party line. We also reveal our own perspectives, summarized above. Then we show a series of five slides, all of Buddhas in sexual embrace.

The reaction is always the same. The audience grasps the idea of the union between compassion and wisdom. But their reactions are much more complex than that. These ordinary Western people see that each of these images is different from the other, in subtle but gripping ways. They understand that there is warmth, beauty, and harmony there. They see sex as the best way to say things about simple, elemental rewards of human life. The imagery brings a catch to their collective throats (including ours), even though they do not know a thing about the doctrines of Buddhism.

Sacred paint has become part of our life. Although we are not collectors by nature, we have Tantric paintings hanging on our walls. The range of human and philosophical themes they encompass startles us. Serenity and ferocity, abstractions and earthiness, clarity and ambiguity, all reach out from these paintings and make us reexamine the fundamentals.

Sacred paint makes us ask, Is my thinking skillful, are my feelings healthy, am I learning to let go of the right things, and am I growing in compassion? Of course, our answers always fall short, but we are grateful that the paint compels the questions.

The Healing Arts

The stream begins on the southern exposure of a high mountain, separating Tibet and Bhutan. Water from melting snow meanders in the lunar landscape and then begins to consolidate in the low places between ridges. The incipient stream drops though terrain too harsh for most living things.

The stream makes a sharp turn to the east and enters a flat place, just 100 yards long. There, it encounters the first signs of people. From time to time, yak herders camp along its edges, seeking shelter in the enclave from the winds and storms of the high country. They come there for a few summer months. Otherwise, the stream and the mountain are a fortress, isolated from the rest of the world by winter weather.

At about 12,000 feet in elevation, the stream begins to flow past permanent human habitations. Farmhouses have been built on ledges along the sides of the valley. In scattered patches, potatoes and buckwheat grow, sustaining human life by a thread.

A bit farther down the slope the first villages appear. In reality, these are just vague aggregations of scattered farmhouses; most are hours' walk from each other. Although people have lived in this part of the valley for centuries, the land cannot support a more dense population. Miniscule fields have been carved into every improbable place. In total, they support a few hundred people.

The valley here is breathtakingly beautiful. Snow-covered Himalayan peaks define the northern horizon. Green hillsides merge into the perfect blue of a high mountain sky. The monasteries, temples, and houses, with their handsome Bhutanese architecture, resonate with the natural wonders of the place.

When we began our journey of learning in Bhutan, we were captured by the backcountry. Traveling in the remote parts of Bhutan felt like coming home. The gracious demeanor of the people, the throat-constricting beauty of the natural surroundings, and the new world of Tantric

Buddhism combined to make these parts of Bhutan the most powerful of magnets.

At the same time, we sensed a dramatic and complex story about health care. Traditionally, lifespans in the valleys were short. Babies and young children died with heartbreaking regularity. Adults suffered one episode after another of trauma and disease. Women experienced respiratory diseases from the dense smoke in their kitchens, and practically everyone was attacked by pathogens in the water.

It is better now, but life in the rural parts of Bhutan is still not easy. Many medical problems are far beyond the capabilities of the local basic health unit. There is no telephone or radio connection with the outside world, and there are no roads. When someone is sick or injured, a runner is sent to seek help, while the outcome hangs in the balance.

As the years went by, we became more focused on health care. We asked: in the countryside of Bhutan, how do the people deal with disease and injury? Who are the health care practitioners, and what do they believe about treating illness and promoting health? What is the impact of Western medicine? Are there elements of Bhutanese health care that could help us live a better life in the West?

The answers are typically Bhutanese—fascinating, and laden with paradox. We begin with an insight a visitor can encounter right away. Find a Bhutanese person who is not feeling well and ask what is wrong. In the West, you would hear an answer that is based on the idea of a "disease entity." It might be as simple as "I have the bug that is going around the office" or as complex as "I have a slipped disk, which is causing both lower back pain and sciatica." In Bhutan, the response is likely to be entirely different, especially if you are in a rural part of the country.

Sometimes, there will be no answer at all. It is as if the Bhutanese person, whose command of English is excellent, suddenly stopped understanding your language. If you manage to shake loose a response, it might be something like this: "There is an evil spirit living in the big rock by the river. The path to my house goes right by the rock, and I am forced to approach that spirit every day. The spirit is making me sick."

Although we often hear about symptoms ("I am sick to my stomach" or "my feet hurt"), we hardly ever hear about disease-entity causes. A well-educated person in the capital city of Thimphu might mention something like "high blood pressure," but it is usually a hesitant and insecure diagnosis. A rural person might not have a single disease-entity word in his or her vocabulary.

When rural people get sick, they turn to lamas, monks, and herbal medicine practitioners for help. These days, they also become customers of basic health units or district hospitals, but in their instincts, the real action lies with traditional health care providers.

When city people get sick, they often go to the hospital, where they receive health care on two parallel tracks. Physicians and nurses trained in Western medicine take care of them. But so do lamas, monks, and herbal medicine practitioners. These two health care teams manage to function side by side, without interfering with each other. As far as we can tell, the patients and their families, in their heart of hearts, are often placing their bets with traditional medicine.

Traditional medicine appears to be grounded in two things: the ancient beliefs about a spirit world and the more formal practices of Tibetan medicine. The sketch "The Spirits Within" explores the spirit realm; here, we will concentrate briefly on Tibetan medicine.

Tibetan medicine began to take shape in the 7th and 8th centuries, when physicians from many parts of Central Asia were invited to Tibet. By the time of the third Dalai Lama, Tibetan medicine had become elaborate and sophisticated and may have been one of the magnets of Tibetan culture that caused Kublai Khan to convert to Buddhism in the 13th century. A hospital and medical college were developed in the Tibetan capital of Lhasa in the 17th century, and a second medical institution was constructed there in the early years of the 20th century. The Chinese destroyed one of the colleges in 1959 (which has since been reestablished in India) but allowed the other to remain. Meanwhile, the precepts of Tibetan medicine remain powerfully entrenched throughout the Tibetan Cultural Area, including Bhutan.

The first thing one notices about Tibetan medicine is its holistic character. Actually, we need a new word to describe Tibetan medicine, because its all-encompassing nature dwarfs anything we describe as "holistic" in the West.

According to the Dalai Lama:

> Tibetan medicine views health as a question of balance. A variety of circumstances such as diet, lifestyle, seasonal and mental conditions can disturb this natural balance, which gives rise to different kinds of disorders.... Health is not a matter of merely personal interest, but a universal concern for which we all share some responsibility. That is why the ideal physician is one who combines sound medical understanding with a strong realization of wisdom and compassion.[16]

The Tantric attitude toward the human body is another feature that has no parallel in the West. In our sketch "Tantra Demystified," you learned about the Tantric Buddhist preoccupation with the body. In contrast to the other major religious traditions, which might tend to treat the body as a distraction, Tantric Buddhism celebrates the body, treating it as the vehicle for spiritual growth and enlightenment. Tantric concepts of channels, energies, and the subtle body are at the basis of Tantric meditational practices.

There is no dividing line between Tantric philosophy and medicine. The same bodily features that form the foundation for spiritual development are at the heart of medicine. It would be like Christians picking up a copy of *Gray's Anatomy* from the racks in the pews in front of them, instead of their hymn books. Within *Gray's*, the material on the central nervous system would be just as important for the Sunday morning examination of the inner life as it would be for treating disease.

In the West, most of us are specialists; it is hard to imagine a culture in which the highest achievement is a comprehensive blending of knowledge and wisdom into a unified vision of life. But that is exactly what is attempted in Tibetan medicine.

Interestingly, the abstractions of Tibetan medicine are easier for a Western person to accept than the details. When Tibetan medicine is described at the highest level, it sounds like a universal blueprint for good health. But the specifics of this medical tradition are hard for many of us Westerners to visualize.

For an example of Tibetan medicine at the abstract level, consider this synopsis from *The Tibetan Art of Healing* by Ian A. Baker:

In Tibetan Medicine, disease in its most pervasive and chronic form is attributed to a basic ignorance of the interdependent origin of all phenomena and the true nature of self. From this primal ignorance arise desire and aggression which betray, respectively, feelings of incompleteness and inner poverty and a deluded sense of threat and separation. Such mental confusion creates physiological stress and thus gives rise to states of inner imbalance. In the words of Dr. Lobsang Rapgay: "Though the mind cannot directly produce physical form, negative feelings such as envy, hatred and fear, when they become habitual, are capable of starting organic changes within our bodies."

Although Tibetan medicine acknowledges the influence of pathogens, improper diet and behaviour in creating disease, the forces of grasping and aggression rooted in human ignorance are considered the three primordial afflictions from which all others stem. According to the medical Tantras, "there is but one cause for disease—the ignorance of not understanding the absence of an abiding self-identity.... Even when a bird soars in the sky, it is not parted from its shadow. Likewise, even when human beings live with joy, with ignorance they are never free of illness."[17]

How could there be a vision of health care with more universal appeal than that? The details of Tibetan medicine, however, are another story. They transport a Western person to a realm of science that might be from another planet. Whether they will be comfortable for you depends on your intellectual flexibility, your left brain/right brain orientation, and your hunger for an alternative theory of health care.

Here, we attempt a summary of a subject that could easily be a lifetime study. The human body is thought to contain three "humours." The English translations for these words probably convey misleading connotations, but we are stuck with them. They are: wind, bile, and phlegm. If the humours function harmoniously, a person enjoys good health. If disharmony arises, that person becomes predisposed toward illness.

Next, we encounter the strong connection with Tantric meditational practices. Each of us has a "subtle body," which begins at our navel. Subtle energy channels flow throughout the body—in total, there are 72,000 of them. There are five channel wheels that link them together, situated at the genitals, heart, throat, navel, and crown of the head. A large part of Tibetan medicine (as well as "unexcelled yoga") relates to the proper management of energy flowing through the channels.

Tibetan medicine holds that there are four kinds of disease. One arises because of bad actions in a past life. Another is caused by spirits. Yet another is a disease that disappears spontaneously, without treatment. The fourth is the only one that is vaguely similar to the Western idea of disease: illnesses caused by the imbalance of the humours, which is in turn brought about by unwise behavior, pathogens, and stresses of the environment.

Practitioners of Tibetan medicine do not use the diagnostic technologies of Western medicine. Instead, they rely on personal and detailed interpretations of a patient's pulse and urine. For a Western person, the scope of pulse examination is startling. Tibetan physicians can determine, from the pulse alone, the patient's physical, emotional, and spiritual well-being. Furthermore, the pulse conveys information about the patient's past lives, the remaining years in this life, and future events in general.

The foregoing descriptions of Tibetan medicine at the abstract and detailed levels leaves many of us Westerners in a pickle. One the one hand, we are intensely interested in more holistic ways of promoting health and treating disease. Our part of the world is fed up with many aspects of Western medicine, including the emphasis on intervention rather than prevention, overspecialization, and the detached, inhumane attitude of many health care professionals. Given those predispositions, Tibetan medicine, at the most abstract levels, creates immediate resonances in many of us.

On the other hand, some of us are perplexed by Tibetan interpretations of anatomy, diagnosis, and treatment. Most of us do not know what to make of the subtle body, or channels, or the importance of phlegm, or physicians who can predict future events by feeling our pulses.

In Bhutan these days, traditional health care, in all of its glorious complexity, seems to be alive and well at the level of the religious professionals and common citizens. The government, however, appears to be emphasizing Western models of medicine. The country's Eighth Five-Year Plan, for example, has an entire chapter devoted to standard Western health care concerns, including primary and secondary care, reproductive health, transport and communication, laboratory services, nutrition, drugs, and initiatives aimed at TB, respiratory infections, diarrheal diseases, leprosy, eye care, and malaria. Traditional health care is mentioned only briefly.[18]

One look at Bhutan's health care data will tell you why. In 1984, Bhutan's infant mortality rate was 142 per 1,000 births. Ten years later, it dropped to half that. In the same period, life expectancy in Bhutan rose from 48 to 66 years. Similar gains occurred in many other health-status indicators. All of this came about from the introduction of Western approaches to health care, including physicians, nurses, hospitals, and basic health units based on Western models. Taken at face value, Bhutan's data seem to suggest that Western medicine has been much more successful at preserving life and improving health than traditional health care.

In the realm of health care, will Bhutan find itself on the slippery slope of Westernization? Is traditional health care at risk?

We do not think so. In spite of the health care data, which give a boost to Western models of medicine, and in spite of the Five-Year Plan's emphasis on Western health care, we believe that the concepts of traditional medicine are fundamental to Bhutan's culture. The precepts of traditional health care are seamlessly interwoven with the Tantric understanding of the world. As long as Bhutan's sense of cultural identity remains strong, traditional health care will survive as well.

In a perfect world, we would invite Bhutanese health care workers to our nearest city, Eugene, Oregon. We are lucky to have a splendid hospital downtown, which might make the Bhutanese feel their current concentration on Western models of health care is the right thing to do. But our visitors would soon discover how many of us are unhappy about our models of medicine. They would find that their talents for combining spiritual and physical healing are exactly what we need. We would learn life-changing insights from them, and they would return home with a renewed sense of confidence about their struggle to combine the old with the new.

The stream reaches the far side of the valley and resumes its descent. It gathers strength and becomes a river that must be crossed with suspension bridges. As the river approaches the border with India, it passes through the turbines of a hydroelectric plant and spends a brief time in the untouched jungles of Southern Bhutan. Then, it enters the India plain. In the country of its birth, this was a simple and pristine high mountain stream. The outside world seeks to alter the stream in every dimension. Many of its attributes will change, but one hopes that the stream's essential character will persist.

Wheel of Law

The Wheel of Law is found in countless temples and monasteries. It symbolizes many things, but one of the most important is the cycle of birth and rebirth.

A World of Circles

In January, Oregon's McKenzie River Valley is a nasty place. In front of our log house, the river rages by, full of mud and high-water debris. Sometimes, after a big rain, trees 200 feet long shoot down the river like freight trains. The Douglas fir forest is cold, squishy, and lifeless. Evenings spent in front of the fireplace are cozy at first, but steadily more confining. We wrestle with cabin fever.

At the very time we are becoming grouchy, something remarkable is happening. In the dankest mud puddles, bright yellow flowers are emerging. These huge blooms of skunk cabbage are the season's first reminder that life will go on, that in just a month or two every square inch of this place will be covered with flora celebrating spring. In Asia, our friends venerate the lotus because it reminds them that mud can give birth to higher planes of life. In Oregon, a much humbler plant does the same thing for us.

By May, the greens are so intense that they hurt your eyes. The McKenzie River calms down and begins to sparkle in the sunlight. Goldfinches zoom in little clouds through the forest, and osprey call overhead. Wild iris spring up along forest roads.

Summer in this region makes us pinch ourselves. The forest has transformed itself into a lovely, cool place, full of mosses and the gargantuan shapes of old-growth firs and cedars. In the subtle light of early morning, deer, elk, and bear make their livings in high-country meadows. The lava in the McKenzie Pass winds among islands of trees that survived volcanic floods in recent geologic times.

Fall changes the texture and colors of our valley. Vine maples turn bright red, making punctuation marks against black lava. Big leaf maples morph into bright yellow. For a little while, wild huckleberries become premium targets for busy fingers. The water of the McKenzie River becomes calm and crystalline. Fly rods get busy, relishing the best fishing of the year.

Our sense of the seasons is, of course, shared by all humans, no matter where they live. In fact, circular periodicity may be the single most powerful unifying factor among earth's tribes. The 24-hour cycle of night and day, the monthly changes of the moon, and the annual passage of seasons are the essential timekeepers for all of us. We live in a world of circles.

Yet Western people may not think in the same way that the natural world is organized. Our minds tend to work in straight lines. We follow career paths, climb social ladders, implement business plans, diagnose illnesses, and design airplanes in sequential steps, each one of which is hooked logically to its predecessor. Even our religious cosmologies are linear. Our religions posit two realms: this life and the afterlife. One is the beginning and the other is the end. They do not repeat themselves.

For an utterly different view of things, one could take a trip to Bhutan. There, Tibetan Buddhism enmeshes you in circles. Circularity, in that tradition, is dominant. Three examples come to mind—the mandala, the Wheel of Law, and the Wheel of Life.

Of the three, only the mandala has become well known in Western culture. In fact, the mandala, especially as it is used in the Kalachakra rite of initiation, has become trendy. Many of us have now seen images of Tibetan monks painstakingly creating sand paintings of the Kalachakra mandala. Some Westerners talk about going through the Kalachakra initiation as if it were similar to paying a visit to the mechanic to get the car tuned up. If you visit your town's Saturday market, you might find a mandala vendor in the booth next to the seller of crystals.

Although the term "mandala" means circle in Sanskrit, it is actually a weak example of the theme of this sketch. The mandala does not directly deal with temporal circularity; that is, it does not symbolize the recycling of life over long periods of time. Instead, a mandala of the Kalachakra kind is a palace. It is the dwelling place of a deity. The mandala serves as the object of meditation and is used by those few people who have mastered the daunting challenges of visualization. The rest of us might admire the artwork, but we may not have enough time and energy remaining in this life to use the mandala for its true purpose.

In contrast, the Wheel of Law is an excellent example of our theme. The wheel seems to be in every temple and monastery you visit in Bhutan (in the form of a stone sculpture). But compared to the painted images on the walls, it may seem tame, so you might not notice it. Generally, the wheel has eight spokes, symbolizing the Buddhist ethical system called the eightfold path. On both sides of the wheel kneel two deer.

Buddhism organizes Buddha's teachings into three groupings, and each of those is called a "turning of the wheel." In its entirety, the thinking represented by the three turnings is complex. Fortunately, there is a simple way of looking at the wheel that is adequate for the theme of this sketch. The Wheel of Law symbolizes endless birth and rebirth. It is a reminder that this life is just a grain of sand among thousands of past and future lives. It suggests that the quality of this life controls, through the concept of karma, the nature of the next one. And the wheel is a call to action, to strip away illusion and achieve enlightenment.

The Wheel of Law is austerely symbolic. Not so with the Wheel of Life. It is normally a wall painting, which is an exuberant collection of pictures. Both wheels are road maps of Buddhist cosmology, but their modes of expression are entirely different. To us, the Wheel of Life seems more characteristic of Bhutan's Tantric Buddhism, with its love of color and graphics.

During our first visits to Bhutan, we encountered Wheels of Life at every turn, but they just seemed to be one graphic among many. Now, we find them riveting. Somehow, a single work of art captures an entire system of thinking. The Wheel of Life reminds us of all we have learned in Bhutan and how diligently we need to work on what remains.

Even though the Wheel of Life documents the entire cosmos, it does not deal with creation. There is nothing in the Wheel, nor in Buddhism as a whole, that resembles "In the beginning, God created the heavens and the earth." We Westerners are used to the idea of a single primal force that was, and is, the architect of the universe. The Bhutanese have no problems with the idea of a transcendental being, but they do not spend much time worrying about creation, and they probably cannot imagine a universe with only one deity.

The Wheel of Life has a strong sense of upstairs/downstairs to it. In the lower part of the wheel are nasty realms for people who have led evil lives. As you rise up the wheel, you pass through places that are increasingly pleasant, known as the realms of hungry ghosts, common animals, human beings, spirits, and gods. The law of karma causes people to be reborn in these places, depending on the quality of their prior lives.

In our opinion, the Wheel of Life operates on two levels. The perimeter of the Wheel consists of 12 vignettes illustrating the Buddha's most important insight, which we Westerners often call "dependent co-arising." This is the Wheel's abstract, philosophical level (and, after some study, became the most rewarding level for us). The inner part of the Wheel functions on a more popular level, documenting the relationship between good deeds (or "merit") and the rewards in subsequent lifetimes. The inner part of the wheel might be oriented toward the karmic aspects of Buddhism, while the outer part might be more strongly focused on personal enlightenment.

Any Western person who has some knowledge of Dante's *Inferno* will immediately see similarities. Both the Wheel of Life (at the karmic level) and the *Inferno* are vivid portraits of the correlation between the moral quality of this life and the comforts of the next one. Both have a multiplicity of hell realms, in which "sinners" suffer fates that are the just desserts for their moral turpitude. In some ways, the *Inferno* carries the symbolism of the circle even further than the Wheel, since each of the *Inferno*'s levels of hell is itself a circle.

The Wheel is a more complete map than the *Inferno* because it documents both the upper and lower levels of the next life. But down there in hell, these Western and Asian cosmologies seem to be cousins.

However, a little reflection reveals some fascinating differences, which may give clues about distinctions between our two cultures that still exist in the 21st century.

First, the very idea of "sin" is different. The center of the Wheel of Life sets out the Buddhist version of sin. There, three animals (the bird, snake, and pig) respectively symbolize ignorance, attachment, and anger. These "sins" are not violations of laws established by a higher power. Instead, they are delusions, or mental errors. Buddhists would say that they are examples of unskillful living.

In contrast, the *Inferno* has a seemingly endless list of wrongdoings, each of which is a violation of a rule established by God and his messengers. The occupants of hell are organized in a hierarchy, with the more reprehensible ones appearing in lower levels of hell:

First level—virtuous people who lived before the time of Jesus, or who were never baptized

Second level—the lustful

Third level—the gluttonous

Fourth level—those who either hoarded or wasted their money

Fifth level—the wrathful

Sixth level—heretics

Seventh level—the violent

Eight and ninth levels—the fraudulent

You could say that the *Inferno*'s idea of sin is "top down," in the sense that wrongdoing is defined by laws established by a supremely powerful, transcendental being. You might also say that the vision of sin in the Wheel of Life is "bottom up," because sin is seen as unwise choices made by individual persons.

Another difference leaps out. The *Inferno* is utterly intolerant of those who are not Christian or of those whose Christianity did not fully adhere to the details of the Christian sect then in power. Heretics are placed in extremely miserable circumstances in the sixth level. Even some of history's most admirable people, such as Homer and Virgil, land in hell because they had the misfortune to live before the time of Jesus. Their punishment for this oversight is to be bitten continuously by flies and wasps.

The Wheel of Life gives no hints of intolerance. The occupants of the lower realms got there because they failed to train their minds and lead skillful lives, not because they joined the wrong religious sect.

The most important difference of all has to do with circles. Dante's hell is forever. The occupants of the hell realms are damned to their harrowing fates in perpetuity. But the whole idea of the Wheel of Life is that it is a dynamic road map. No one is stuck in the lower realms forever. Everyone has the chance to live a future life of greater merit and thus rise to a higher level.

If you look closely at the portraits of the three hell realms in the Wheel, you will see the Buddha in all of them. In the realm of the hungry ghosts, he carries a box full of jewels of the mind. In the lowest hell realm, he carries the flame of hope. And in the realm of animals, the Buddha has a book. The message, in all cases, is that even the most destitute of sentient beings have an opportunity, through rebirth, to live more meritorious lives and to improve their lots.

Earlier in this sketch we mentioned that the Wheel of Life has moved to the center of our learning experience in Bhutan. The preceding paragraphs begin to explain why. But there is another aspect of the Wheel that makes it remarkably powerful for Western people.

The Wheel of Life can be interpreted as a "physical" cosmology in the same way that heaven and hell are elements of a physical cosmology for Christians. It is just as valid to look at the Wheel of Life as a psychological template, in which concepts like heaven and hell are metaphors for our inner lives. Furthermore, it is perfectly acceptable to interpret the multiple lives depicted by the Wheel as chapters in this life. Thus within a single life, each of us can ascend, or descend, into the various realms of the Wheel on the basis of how skillfully we have lived and how well we have trained our minds.

This feature of the Wheel of Life was fresh air for us. We, like many other Westerners, are not sure what to do with the concept of reincarnation. Not that we argue with it. But because of our upbringing, it is a concept that does not come naturally. In turn, our indecision sometimes makes it difficult to appreciate aspects of Buddhism that depend on a literal and unquestioning belief in reincarnation.

The Wheel of Life, however, gave us the freedom to appreciate Buddhism in terms of this life. And once we started down that path, we found the Wheel endlessly insightful. We owe this turning point to friends in Bhutan who, in their gentle, kind way, opened our eyes.

These days, we find that we are thinking not so much about the heaven/hell portraits in the center of the wheel, but about the "preconditions" illustrated in the Wheel's perimeter. In effect, these 12 vignettes confront us with the question, How do I train my mind to cut back on my attachments and achieve a modest degree of enlightenment?

Now, when we visit Bhutan, we try to sense how the circular view of life affects the day-to-day texture of the place. Sometimes, it is obvious. For example, one often hears an older person say, "I need to stay close to home this year, preparing for the next life." And circularity is plainly visible in the Bhutanese attitude toward the environment, where the people view themselves as stewards for future generations, rather than consumers seeking the gain of the moment. (See the sketch "Caring for the Earth.")

More often, however, the world of circles is a subtle thing—in small scenes, like a Bhutanese person's refusal to kill a rat that has invaded the bathroom, or the fluttering of prayer flags whose purpose is to help a deceased person cross over to the next life. Most of all, you see the world of circles in the restraint and gentleness of the Bhutanese personality, which is the very opposite of "you only live once, so grab it all."

As each new season passes on the McKenzie River, we sense that we have changed one more notch. It took some help from friends half a world away, but we might be making halting progress. These days, three prayer flags stand in the forest, just a few feet from the river. We are not sure we are responding to them in exactly the right way, but they whisper these things to us: let go of attachments, live compassionately, search for the next life, even within this one.

CARING FOR THE EARTH

That morning, we had taken a long walk in the Gantey Valley. Ahead of us, shrouded by wisps of fog, the Gantey Gompa emerged to glow in the sunlight for a moment or two, then faded to gray. The morning light, shaped by its long journey through the atmosphere, painted the houses with shades of yellow and rose. Sounds of Gantey Village awakening encompassed us, each one crystalline, dwelling in the quiet morning air.

The day before, we had talked about a half-formed dream. Do you think it might be possible, we had asked each other, to build a retreat house in the valley? In the manner of the best dreams, we imagined rooms, spaces, vistas that could quiet the inner self. We felt a stirring of hope that we might begin to find a pathway to wisdom in the Himalayas. During our walk, the dream breathed in and out, at one moment taking on concrete dimensions, and at another fading to a sense of fantasy. Later, home in Oregon, and in the course of ordinary life, the dream died—a victim of long distances, practical complications, and, we suppose, lack of courage or imagination. But for a moment, Gantey, through its extraordinary setting and suffused spirituality, had given us a lens that felt wonderfully uplifting.

Sonam Jatso and Karma Lotey had stayed behind for a few hours, both of them claiming that they preferred a lazy start that morning. But we sensed it was another case of the inexhaustible Bhutanese sensitivity. Knowing that we would appreciate some solitude in that uncommon place, they elegantly gave us the space and time. Just before we reached the Gantey Gompa, we heard a sound behind us. Sonam and Karma had arrived, ready to give us a lift.

In our experience, most magical times are short, an hour or two. That day was different, with the spell carrying us over the edge of the valley's rim and into primeval forest. Even at this high altitude, Bhutan's forest was an astonishing tapestry of living things. We rounded a corner and then Karma's voice gave us goose bumps—gray langurs, straight ahead! Sonam stopped the car and we watched a troop of monkeys, at least 20, moving sinuously down the slope to the edge of the road. We and the langurs quietly shared that moment in the forest. Briefly, we captured the sense of being part of the community of sentient beings, of a wheel of existence in which we, the monkeys, and the forest were partners in the continuum of life. A gift of Bhutan's unspoiled environment.

Practically every visitor to Bhutan has a similar story. Bhutan's environmental treasure house is a showstopper. No matter how many times you return, the backcountry of Bhutan has you in its grip.

Yet Bhutan is an implausible place for humans. It is a staircase ascending the southern slope of the Himalayas, from the Indian plain (barely above sea level) to mountain peaks, edging Tibet at 26,000 feet. The land has been uplifted, creased, and eroded into a quilt of valleys and ridges. For centuries, people struggled from one valley to the next, spending days on isolated, dangerous tracks to travel a few horizontal miles. One by one, they uncovered and farmed Bhutan's patches of arable land.

Before 1961, there were virtually no roads, schools, doctors, or electricity. Half of the children born in Bhutan died at birth or a few years later. Smallpox, cholera, malaria, respiratory diseases, and leprosy were common.

In a twist of fate, the things that made Bhutan difficult for people shaped and preserved the natural world. A geography that was often cruel to human life gave rise to a multitude of microhabitats, in turn leading to biodiversity among the plants and animals. That geography also restrained human consumption of natural resources by keeping the British out of Bhutan, defending against invaders from Tibet, and restricting Bhutan's own growth in population. The results: an underpopulated corner of Asia with an abundance of natural resources.

The wilderness of Bhutan inspires the wonderment recalled by the explorers of the New World: landscapes of dark green trees roll toward the horizon in every direction. Tropical jungles, mid-altitude forests, and alpine landscapes house animals that usually appear in children's storybooks: snow leopards, yaks, red pandas, takins, golden langur monkeys, tigers, and rhinos. Bhutan's ecosystem includes an estimated 7,790 species of birds, 50 species of rhododendron, 200 species of mammals, and 2,000 species of plants—all this in an area about one tenth the size of California.

Three hundred species of plants and animals are used to make more than 200 kinds of traditional medicines. Diverse products from the natural world provide the people, 85 percent of whom live in rural areas, with construction materials, food, fiber, and fuel. Healthy and complex ecosystems stabilize Bhutan's steep slopes, protect the water supply, recycle nutrients, control pests, and provide pollination for crops.

Bhutan's biodiversity is important for the rest of us. Eighty percent of our medicines come from the natural world. Our domestic livestock and crops depend on their wild analogues for improvement and diversification. With Bhutan's store of untouched genetic resources, "bioprospecting" (the search for new genes for the pharmaceutical, biotechnology, and agricultural industries) may become one of the country's most important sources of export earnings.

Bhutan's well-preserved environment contrasts starkly with other parts of Asia. In one country after another, the themes are discouraging—deforestation, erosion, water and air pollution, and the extinction of living things. Because of their natural courtesy, Bhutanese people are reluctant to criticize their neighbors publicly. But in private conversations, it becomes clear that they are horrified by environmental disasters around them and are trying to steer in a different direction.

What sets Bhutan apart from its neighbors is its willingness to translate environmental laws into action. Many countries have adopted environmental laws, setting aside parks and protected areas, pledging to protect the quality of air and water, and making earnest commitments to forests and wild creatures. But if our traveling experiences are a reasonable barometer, in much of the world, environmental legislation is enforced with a wink of the eye.

In Bhutan, however, environmental policies are serious business. This scene illustrates the point. We had been on the road for two weeks, traveling to remote parts of Eastern Bhutan—a trip that was one of the high points of our lives, but exhausting. Finally, in the obscure light of dusk, we reached the outskirts of Thimphu. Home base within reach! Suddenly, Sonam stopped the car, and we saw in our headlights a line of Tata trucks blocking the road. One at a time, the trucks were being searched for illegally transported logs. A year earlier, new legislation had been passed in Bhutan prohibiting the export of unprocessed forest products. Before us was tangible proof that public environmental policy in this country had survived the perilous journey from legal abstractions to down-to-earth enforcement.

Bhutan has nine national parks, reserves, and sanctuaries that cover more than 26 percent of the country. The government is committed to maintaining at least 60 percent of the land area under forest cover, and this policy is enforced in multiple, vigorous ways. Intense planning is under way to coordinate the development of hydropower, food production, and industrial development with the health of the environment. The scene we witnessed near Thimphu is repeated every day throughout the country.

Until 1990, Bhutan's environmental value system tended to be informal and instinctual. In that year, government officials gathered in the city of Paro and put together an environmental policy called The Paro Resolution on Environment and Sustainable Development. Here is an excerpt from the resolution's preamble:

> This is the challenge of sustainable development: To raise the material well-being of all our citizens and to meet their spiritual aspirations, without impoverishing our children and grandchildren. The key is to find a development path that will allow the country to meet the pressing needs of the people, without undermining the resource base of the economy. New industries, new agricultural markets, and new forestry products need to be carefully developed, with respect to their broader environmental ramifications....
>
> Sustainable development, we believe, is a concept that is in harmony with the cultural and religious traditions of Bhutan. Our nation already has a strong conservation ethic, and indeed, respect for the natural world is a central tenet of Buddhism.... We urge the nation to build on this ancient wisdom, to purse a Middle Path of Development for the Kingdom, and thereby ensure the sustained happiness and prosperity of our people.[19]

These thoughts, particularly those relating to the Buddhist veneration of the natural world, have echoed in our minds. Other Buddhist countries seem to have leveled their forests just as fast as the rest of us. But that has not happened in Bhutan. Why not?

Perhaps these words from our friend Kunzang Dechen provide a hint. We are talking to him about the religious roots for a love of the environment. Kunzang says: "If people deify things in nature, then they aren't out to tarnish nature, but to live in harmony with it. The worship of animals and plant life means giving animals and plant life a higher status—seeing it as a part of yourself, as an extension of yourself. So you don't find you want to exploit nature, you just want to take what is necessary for your needs."

Kunzang then explains that in his childhood, his mother firmly supported the idea that all natural objects have a place and spirit. Kunzang enjoyed skipping stones in a nearby river. He remembers often being reprimanded by his mother, who asked him, "Why do you want to displace those stones from where they are and throw them in the cold river?"

Kunzang's mother has introduced us to the heart of the matter. There are two value systems functioning in Bhutan, side by side. One is the shamanistic worldview that dates as far back as recorded history (which we frequently call "folk religion"). The other is formal Buddhism, which arrived in Bhutan in the 8th century. Both venerate the natural world, and both are vibrantly alive in Bhutan.

In the folk religion, geography is sacred. Mountains are homes to mountain deities, the most terrifying or protective of all the folk deities. Lesser deities dwell in the streams, lakes, rocks, cliffs, trees, and the atmosphere itself. To this day, much of the spiritual life of Himalayans is intended to appease the gods that surround them in the landscape and to enlist their help in the struggle to survive in a risky place. Everywhere in the backcountry of Bhutan, one sees *mani* walls, *chortens*, and rock cairns made by human beings anxious to make peace with gods, spirits, and ghosts.

Even formal planning documents in Bhutan account for places made sacred by the ancient religion. Here are some interesting words from *The Middle Path—National Environment Strategy for Bhutan*:

> In addition to officially protected areas are those that result from unofficial ones. All across the country are distinct topographical features known as *nheys* which have

been left untouched by local populations because they are believed to be the home of local deities or guardians. These *nheys*, which may take the form of mountain lakes, peaks, forest groves, or rocky outcroppings, must be scrupulously avoided. To make sure that these *nheys* are not infringed on...they will need to be officially authenticated and demarcated by the appropriate local authorities.[20]

Formal Buddhism also shapes environmental policy in powerful ways. Here, we think the driving force is the Buddhist conception of reincarnation. As you know from the sketch "A World of Circles," the Bhutanese people believe that this life is just one of many. According to their cosmology, each of us occupies a place on this earth for a long, long time, through a succession of rebirths. We believe that Buddhist ideas about reincarnation encourage Bhutanese people to view themselves as stewards of natural resources, rather than consumers.

Here is an exercise you can try for yourself. Find a quiet place and calm your mind. Picture the rhythms of your existence, ebbing at a moment, flowing at the next. Think of coming into the world alone and leaving it alone. Do your best to give some shape to your time on this planet.

When we do this, we usually have a sense of a beginning and an end. Except for a few unsettling moments in the Himalayas, our imagination does not easily reach into times before our birth. And the end of life, to us, often seems like the end altogether.

Of course, many people in the Western traditions believe in an afterlife. But it seems to be a life vastly removed from daily existence, and apparently it lasts forever. In any event, our traditions do not contemplate that we will return to the gritty complications of this world.

You could say that the Western view of life is linear. Whether or not we go to church or temple, most Westerners understand life on earth as a one-time experience in which we do the best we can with what we have. We live along a line, using human and material resources to achieve the most from our brief existence.

We tend to look at the physical world as a supermarket, and we take all we can afford. "Live it up" we like to say, as we talk ourselves into one form of consumption or another.

Our linear view of life affects our sense of partnership. It is easy for us to interpret family members, friends, business colleagues, and political allies as partners. But do Westerners feel the same way about horseflies, or rattlesnakes, or rainbow trout? And here is an especially revealing test— do we feel a sense of oneness with unborn generations, or with those who are dead, whether they are people or creatures?

Westerners sometimes have an excellent ability to become partners with other living humans, so long as everyone's interests are aligned. But with the exception of animals that evolved specifically to be cute or attractive in the eyes of humans (like dogs and cats), we normally have a limited feeling of alliance with other living creatures. And most of us have no sense of commitment or closeness to previous generations or unborn beings. Our way of expressing this is that Western people can be partners in space (to a limited degree), but not in time.

Bhutanese see things differently. In their view, life moves in a circle. All sentient beings move from one realm of existence to another, living, dying, and reincarnating. In your next life, you could be any one of the millions of species that inhabit the earth. None of us occupies a single life, moving along a straight line. Instead, all of us emerge and reemerge as members of a vast community of sentient beings. We are, therefore, not only partners in space; we are partners in time.

We believe that the circular worldview of formal Buddhism has, in Bhutan at least, shaped attitudes toward the environment. In our time in Bhutan, we have seldom encountered a person with a "grab it now" attitude toward natural resources. Instead, we encounter citizens who naturally look at themselves as the environment's protectors, both for their own generation and generations to come.

Thus the astonishing conservation ethic at work in Bhutan is, we believe, fueled by two belief systems working together. The ancient folk religion produces a kind of visceral awe, reverence, and respect for the natural world. It resides in the right side of the brain and has the power and universality of all intuitive thinking. Formal Buddhism, with its emphasis on the circularity of life, provides a left-sided intellectual polish. Buddhism creates a rational explanation and structure for an environmental sensitivity that was already bred in the bone. Together, they create a breathtaking view of living creatures and sacred geography.

We close this sketch with a scene on a mountainside in Eastern Bhutan. We are departing from a faraway monastery called Rawabi Gompa, and our group is descending a steep trail. Suddenly, the man in front of Russ stops in his tracks. Russ digs his hiking boots into the mud and skids to a stop, barely avoiding a collision. Our friend picks a leaf from a shrub. He bends down and carefully slides the leaf under a spider, no more than half an inch long. When the spider is safely on the leaf, our friend turns to the side of the trail and puts the spider in a secluded place. He resumes his hike down the trail. We imagine the event seemed as natural to him as breathing.

Dorje

The Dorje is most commonly described as a thunderbolt and is one of the most powerful symbols of Tibetan Buddhism. It is frequently associated with the bell. Together, they represent the elaborate male/female principles of this tradition.

Kunley, Where Are You When We Need You?

In Bhutan, there is list of people who are universally admired. You have met many of them in this book—Guru Rinpoche, the Shabdrung, the four kings, to name a few. This sketch introduces you to a new character, one who is closer to the hearts of the people than any other. Drukpa Kunley— 16th-century sage, adventurer, poet, womanizer, lama, and all-around deflator of egos.

We confess at the outset that we love this man. Drukpa Kunley was a genius at detecting and destroying pompous words, dogmatic opinions, institutional hierarchies, and what we now call political correctness. In addition to all that, he had a warm heart, an enthusiastic attitude toward sex, and a commitment to serving the people. He did not give a hoot about the rules, yet he left a constructive legacy that gets stronger as the centuries pass by.

Whenever we are bogged down by the labyrinth of formal Buddhism, or, for that matter, by the events of modern America, we bring Drukpa Kunley to mind. He restores our perspective and makes us feel better.

Kunley was one of a number of roguish characters who are now known as divine madmen, or crazy saints. Divine madmen were famous for their rough ways and insightful commentary. They wandered around the countryside, challenging authority and generally rattling the timbers of the established social order. Divine madmen were generally tolerated by the people. In some cases, particularly in the case of Drukpa Kunley, they were venerated.

Kunley was raised in a monastery, where he received all the normal training of a Tibetan Buddhist monk (of the Kagyu school). According to legend, he achieved "Buddhahood" at a young age and then left the monastery to roam through Tibet and Bhutan in the manner of a crazy saint. Drukpa Kunley divided his time between Tibet and Bhutan but seems to have felt a special affection for the Bhutanese. In Tibet, Drukpa Kunley unearthed endless ways to ridicule authority and challenge social convention. He tended to change focus in Bhutan, spending much of his time conquering demons.

In the same way that Guru Rinpoche subdued demons and converted them to formal Buddhism, Kunley transformed the evil forces of Bhutan. There was, however, a huge difference in style. Guru Rinpoche is always portrayed as serious, sober, and transcendental. Drukpa Kunley did much of the conquering with a penis-headed stick, or with his own penis, which he referred to as the "flaming thunderbolt of wisdom." Kunley could never resist mixing serious religious business with a joke or two.

Kunley's willingness to ridicule the rich and powerful is startling. Seemingly, nothing was off limits. If wanted to scorn the avarice of local landowners or joke about the sexual habits of lamas, he went right ahead. In other cultures, such stern social criticism might lead straight to the gallows. In Tibet and Bhutan, Drukpa Kunley's antics were not only tolerated, but were held in the highest esteem by many.

Although there is no doubt about Kunley's dedication to Buddhist principles, he loved a good time. Whenever he visited a new place, the first words from his mouth generally dealt with drinking and sex. In a flash, Kunley would be making love with a handsome woman, drinking with the boys, and entertaining the crowds with poetry that was bawdy and erudite at the same time.

Drukpa Kunley was especially taken with the beautiful women of Bhutan; to this day, the stories of his escapades in the southern valleys are treasured by Bhutanese women and men alike.

To the best of our knowledge, there is only one book in English about Drukpa Kunley: *The Divine Madman,* by Keith Dowman. It is a gem. (If our sketches motivate you to buy just one book, it should be this one.) All of the quoted passages in this sketch are taken from Dowman. Dowman's translation is based on a Tibetan text compiled in 1966 by Geshey Chaphu, a Bhutanese authority on Drukpa Kunley. A revised version was then prepared by Lopon Nado, which was printed in Kalimpong, India.[21]

We begin with a wonderfully focused confrontation of establishment and anti-establishment. Imagine that Drukpa Kunley is sitting on a rock somewhere in Tibet, sunning his unclothed bottom. A powerful Buddhist official named Sakya Panchen approaches, accompanied by 100 servants.

Sakya Panchen calls out, scolding Kunley for his loose morals. Kunley replies in verse.

> Never knowing any physical discomfort,
>
> Hoping for Buddhahood in coloured robes,
>
> Sending your disciples to hell,
>
> I feel sad to set eyes upon you.
>
> Be on your way, Sakya Panchen, Lord of Beings!
>
> Go! Give your discourses and initiations,
>
> Gather around you your vow violators,
>
> Sow your seeds of disaster,
>
> Grow your shoots of passion,
>
> Ripen your karma of the Bardo,
>
> Carry the songs of old women,
>
> Fulfil your duty to your dependents,
>
> And fill your treasure house with riches!

Sakya Panchen replies, also in verse.

> Here by a cave without door or pillar,
>
> Sits Drukpa Kunley with the dirty mouth
>
> Who babbles nonsense wherever he is.
>
> I feel great pity for you!
>
> Go! Wander the world without purpose,
>
> Destroy the faith of the people you meet,
>
> Carry your wealth on your penis head,
>
> Offer your sacred substance to whores,
>
> Arouse the dogs with your door-knocking,
>
> And break the ribs of the eldest bitches;
>
> Pick your nits and toss them like stones behind you,
>
> Break the hip bones of your women,
>
> And sun-bathe wherever you wish![22]

Here is the best part of this exchange. In a classically Tibetan gesture of tolerance, each is pleased with the verses of the other and their mutual understanding. Sakya Panchen invites Kunley to the monastery and provides him with a horse to ride. Of course, Drukpa Kunley cannot resist teasing some farm girls along the way. When Sakya Panchen grumbles, Kunley replies, "What's the matter? All girls like to get laid."

Another revealing scene takes place at the famous Tibetan monastery of Samye. Drukpa Kunley has arrived during a festival, and the monastery is full of people from all over the country who are performing their religious duties. Drukpa Kunley is asked which religious rites he will perform. Kunley declares that he is too lazy to tackle the usual ceremonies, so he resorts to verse. An old man asks him to recite his thinking on "The Destruction of Evil Forces and Pacification of Obstructing Spirits." Kunley says:

> Preaching the Law with pride and vanity
>
> Is the weakness of scholars and teachers—
>
> Remove it through humility and tranquility....
>
> Attachment to fashionable jewelry
>
> Is the bane of all women—
>
> Remove it by dressing them in patched rags.
>
> The Lama's thick penis
>
> Is the plague of nuns—
>
> Avoid it by shouting to awaken the neighbors.
>
> Mother's long fingernails
>
> Spell disaster to father's balls—
>
> Avert it by cutting her nails with a small sharp knife....
>
> A garrulous gossiping woman
>
> Is a plague on the neighbors—
>
> Avert it by refusing to converse.[23]

Drukpa Kunley goes on, at length, with his trademark mixture of lofty insights and earthy advice. When he finishes, some in the audience call him an idiot and a madman. But the others understand Kunley's poetry was a wondrously fresh tour of religious and practical issues. "Those who folded their hands in reverence were filled with faith."

Imagine now that we are on the road to a place in Tibet called Ralung. We stop to gossip with some travelers and hear the story of Drukpa Kunley's encounter with an old man who was carrying a rolled up painting known as a *thangka*, to be blessed by a Buddhist big wig. The *thangka* was well done, but lacked the usual final touches made from gold.

> Show me your scroll, said the lama. The old man gave it to him, asking his opinion of the work. "Not bad at all," the Lama told him, "but I can improve it like this." And he took out his penis and urinated over the painting.
>
> The old man was shocked speechless, but finally managed to say, "Apau! What have you done, you madman?" And he began to cry.
>
> The Lama rolled up the wet scroll and calmly returned it to the old man. "Now take it for the blessing," he said.
>
> When the old man reached Ralung he was granted audience.... "I painted this...thangka to gain merit," he told the abbot, "and I have brought it to you for your blessing. But on the way I met a madman who urinated on it and ruined it. Here it is. Please look at it."
>
> [The abbot] opened it and saw where the urine had splashed was now shining with gold. "There is no need for my blessing," he told the old man. "It has already been blessed in the best possible way." The old man gained unsurpassable faith and gave loud thanksgiving.[24]

We will transport ourselves to another spot in Tibet by the name of Kaklha Gampo. Drukpa Kunley has just arrived, finding a crowd of lay and professional monks undertaking religious ritual. Along the way, Kunley has flirted nonstop with the local girls. His come-ons are direct, to say the least.

> It would seem by the size of your buttocks,
>
> That your nature is exceedingly lustful.
>
> It would seem from your thin, pert mouth,

That your muscle is tight and strong.

It would seem from your legs and muscular thighs,

That your pelvic-thrust is particularly efficient.

Let's see how you perform![25]

When Drukpa Kunley settles down for serious discourse with the assembled monks and nuns, he is asked who are the most pious persons he has met during his wanderings. Do not be concerned about the names of the various orders of Tibetan Buddhism. The substance of Kunley's commentary will be clear.

> I, an ever roaming [crazy saint], visited a Kahgyu Academy,
>
> And in that Kahgyu every monk was holding a jug full of chung—
>
> So fearful of becoming a drunken reveller, I kept to myself.
>
> I, an ever roaming [crazy saint], visited a Sakya Academy,
>
> And in that Sakya Academy the monks were splitting subtle doctrinal hairs—
>
> So fearful of forsaking the true path of [Buddhism], I kept to myself.
>
> I, an ever roaming [crazy saint], visited the Academy of Galden,
>
> And in the Galden Academy each monk was seeking a boyfriend—
>
> So fearful of losing my semen, I kept to myself....
>
> I, an ever roaming [crazy saint] visited Mountain Hermitages,
>
> And in those hermitages the monks were gathering worldly possessions—
>
> So fearing to break my vows to my Lama, I kept to myself....
>
> I, an ever roaming [crazy saint] visited a Retreat Centre,
>
> And here the meditators basked in the sun—

So fearing to relax in a small hut's security, I kept to
 myself....

I, an ever roaming [crazy saint] visited the Religious
 Centre of Lhasa,

Where the hostesses were hoping for their guests' gifts
 and favors—

So fearing to become a flatterer, I kept to myself.

I, an ever roaming [crazy saint] wandering throughout the
 land,

Found self-seeking suffers wherever I looked—

So fearful of thinking only of myself, I kept to myself.[26]

Our next Kunley story is a beauty. It takes place near Thimphu, the
capital of modern Bhutan. A serpent demon had declared war on the
people, carrying them off at night. Only one old woman remained; the
serpent demon and his buddies were determined to eat her too.

Demons were Drukpa Kunley's speciality. He paid the old woman a
visit; she told him to flee before he was eaten alive. The woman was certain she would not live through the night. She asked Kunley to return to
her house after her death and to distribute her things to the poor. Kunley
told her not to worry. He would stay with her during the night. As usual,
he asked for *chaang* (the local booze, also known as *chung*).

He was drinking when night fell and the demons arrived
at the door. When they began pounding upon it the old
woman began screaming in paroxysms of fear.

"You stay up here," the Lama directed. "I'll take care
of this." Down below, he took his erect penis in his hand
and thrust it through the hole in the door which was
big enough to take a fist and as a Flaming Thunderbolt
of Wisdom it rammed into the Serpent Demon's gaping
red mouth knocking out four teeth above and four teeth
below.

"Something hit me in the mouth!" screamed the demon
wildly, and fled down the terraces of the river valley until
he came to the cave called Lion Victory-Banner, where a

nun called Lotus Samadhi was sitting deep in meditation.…"Something weird hit me in the mouth," he stormed breathlessly.

"Well, what was it, and where did it come from?" she enquired.

"It was at the old woman of Gomsarhka's house. A strange man who was neither a layman nor a monk hit me with a flaming iron hammer," panted the demon.

"You have been hit by a magical device," the nun told him. "That kind of wound never heals. If you doubt me, look at this." She raised her skirt and opened her legs. "This wound was caused by the same weapon. There is no way to heal it."

The demon put his finger to it and raised it to his nose. "Akha! kha! This wound has gone putrid and I suppose mine will go the same way," he moaned. "What should I do?"[27]

The nun tells the demon that he has encountered Drukpa Kunley. She instructs him to go back to the house. "Offer him your life, and vow never to harm living creatures again. Then perhaps you may be cured." So, the demon returns to the house, prostrates himself before Kunley, and offers Kunley his life. Kunley places his Thunderbolt of Wisdom on the demon's head and ordains him as a protector of formal Buddhism.

Reading the adventures of Drukpa Kunley makes our heads spin. Nothing in our upbringing prepared us for this roller coaster between the bawdy and the sacred. We have, however, become devoted fans. Not only are Kunley's escapades rewarding in themselves, they stir up gripping questions about our culture.

We could be wrong, but we do not think that the formal American institutions contain safety valves remotely similar to the crazy saints. Do the churches, temples, or mosques in this country empower people to unmask the arrogance of leadership? Do our universities or our city, state, or federal governments authorize anyone to ridicule hypocrisy or sanctimony? Does contrarian commentary always have to come from without, in late night television or the op-ed pages, or is it ever encouraged to come from within?

These days, when we watch certain politicians huff and puff, or listen to certain institutional leaders drone on about political correctness, we cannot keep the image of Drupka Kunley from our minds. Kunley, we had to go a long way to find you, but thank heavens we did.

Is Sex Necessary?

Bhutanese may be the most polite, demur human beings on earth. These people define the very idea of modesty, from their conservative, formal clothing to their soft-spoken and self-effacing manner. But the reality of Bhutanese culture is much more complex and interesting than that. As you get to know the culture, you catch glimpses of a fascinating paradox. In your lifetime, you have never seen the likes of it—a cautious, conservative nation that is, at the same time, earthy beyond your imagination.

Every time we think about sexuality in Bhutan, we go around in the most amusing intellectual circles. Sometimes, we throw up our hands and think of our hero James Thurber and the quote we have used for the title of this sketch.

Please imagine that you are in Bumthang during the annual Fire Festival. It is nighttime, and a throng of people has crowded into the grounds of the Jamphel Lhakhang, surrounding dancers who move between shadows and firelight. Golds and reds and blacks make soft, hypnotic circles in the night. Then, Atsara the clown! At first obscure in the shadows, and then right in front of you, Atsara works the crowd, his red mask, fierce nose, and nonstop antics entertaining the people. And clutched in both hands is a wooden penis. Atsara waves his penis at the crowd in the manner of a conductor leading the Presto movement of a symphony. The people laugh and giggle with the delight of children at a circus.

To our ears, there is not one lascivious note. That huge penis seems to bring forth a cheerful, natural kind of amusement. Not self-conscious, not dirty, and not in conflict with the religion or values of the culture. Just plain fun.

So it goes in Bhutan. This country makes you think about sex differently.

The June 1999 issue of *New Yorker* magazine included an article about Bhutan, innocently titled "Fertile Ground." The author does not waste time getting to her topic. In her first sentence, she says: "The penises of Bhutan amazed me, there were so many of them."

We do not respect the tone of the *New Yorker* article, but there is no denying that sexual symbols are at every turn. Farm houses are decorated by enormous penises painted on the exterior walls, doorways feature stylized vaginas, and roofs often have little wooden phalluses hanging from their corners. Atsara the clown, with his impressive appendage, is probably the favorite figure in religious festivals. Paintings and bronze renderings of the *vajra* are seen everywhere—at one level, they are interpreted as a thunderbolt, at another, as the male organ. And the lotus, the most widespread symbol in a vast part of Asia, is sometimes seen as enlightenment growing out of the mud of ordinary existence, and at others as a vagina.

An easy way to get a laugh in Bhutan is to crack a joke about sex. Notice that we did not say a dirty joke, because sexual humor in this country does not normally have a nasty tinge to it. In the right time and place, both men and women love straightforward, cheerfully explicit joshing about sex. (You will recall the raunchy teasing that the dancing girls dish out during archery matches.)

This is a country where sexuality often operates in an easygoing environment. Extramarital sex is common. Marriage is often an informal arrangement, especially for rural people. Both men and women are free to divorce whenever they want to.

Here is a memorable example of sexuality in Bhutan. It is called "night hunting."

In the remote parts of the country (which includes most of it), boys and girls need a way to get to know each other. They can meet at religious festivals, but otherwise they need to spend most of their time with the rigorous chores of a farm. When night falls, the people, in the manner of farm people across the world, go to bed. Not the boys. They have missions that can only take place in the cover of darkness.

The boys sneak out of their houses and fan out across the countryside. They head toward houses of girls who have caught their fancy. Each boy carries a knife whose main purpose is to pry open doors and windows.

Quiet as mice, the boys sneak up to the houses, open doors and windows, and crawl inside. Then the hard part begins. Somehow, the boys need to maneuver through a pitch-black, unfamiliar place, finding the girl and avoiding family members. And then comes an even harder part. The male persons must devise ways to entertain the female persons all night long, without making a sound.

When the festivities are over, the boys crawl outside, relatch doors and windows, and take the long hike back home. They arrive just before the sun comes up and just before it is time to spend another long day in the fields.

Sometimes night hunting does not go smoothly. Boys have been known to crawl into the beds of their sweethearts' fathers. Even in easygoing Bhutan, that is regarded as a serious error. Boys caught in this embarrassing situation make an exit in the fastest possible manner.

Perhaps the most heartening aspect of night hunting is its linkage to marriage. It is hard to see how this is possible, but a boy and girl in a night-hunting episode are not only able to perform the full range of sexual functions in secrecy, they are also able to discuss the possibility of marriage. If marriage is agreed upon, then sometimes the boy simply stays in the house. The sun comes up, the family finds him in the house, and, with a minimum of fuss, the two are regarded as man and wife.

Sexuality is plainly visible in the urban parts of Bhutan as well. Memorial Chorten in the capital city of Thimphu is a good example. This is a relatively modern place, built in 1974 in honor of Bhutan's third king. It is one of our favorite places to visit in Thimphu because it is around the corner from the place we stay, and no other site in Bhutan so dramatically illustrates the powerful role of sexuality in Tantric Buddhism.

Memorial Chorten is three stories high, with an internal staircase connecting each of the floors. The interior is jammed with statues of wrathful deities and their female consorts. Most of the figures are larger than life-size, and all of them are in full sexual embrace. One day we got curious and counted 36 couples.

To most Westerners, this place is a jaw-dropper. It is entertaining to find a quiet corner in Memorial Chorten and watch the reaction of Western people when they first figure out what is going on. It is even more interesting to watch the reactions of monks from other parts of Asia who are visiting Memorial Chorten for the first time. They get just as sheepish and disconcerted as those of us from the West.

Another intriguing example of sex in Bhutan comes from archery. The first match we attended (in the Western Bhutan town of Ha) started with the usual solemn prayer ceremony and circle dances, but beneath the decorum a joke was forming that took us hours to recognize. Striking the target is so difficult that some players will try for hours before they finally get a hit. Just about lunch time, we noticed that some of the players had received awards, which were hanging from their belts. At first, we thought the best players were being honored; then we realized these were the players who were really struggling. "What's that, Karma?" we asked, in our innocence. Karma looked sheepish, and then came closer so we could get a better look. Hanging from Karma's belt and, indeed, from the belts of many other players, was a carved wooden penis. Karma was stuck with the darn thing until he got a hit.

When a player gets a hit, he is awarded a sash, which he hangs from his belt. Thus Karma and his cohorts were waiting for the magic moment, when they could exchange a sash for the booby prize. A talented player accumulates so many sashes that they circle his body, making him look like an Asian version of a hula dancer. According to tradition, players with that many sashes are required to remove their *ghos* and to dance for the crowd with nothing on but the sashes. We have never seen that happen, but it seems consistent with the sense of humor that otherwise prevails at archery matches.

While the shooting is going on, players from the two teams stand next to the targets at both ends of the field. That is a natural thing to do from the "shooting" end of the field, but it is alarming at the "receiving" end. The arrows come whistling in just four or five feet away from the players, who are busy with their joking, teasing, and other important matters of the day. However, when one of their teammates gets a hit, the players spring into action. They rush to the target and join in a circle dance. They sing as they dance, usually fragments of popular love songs, or songs intended especially for archery.

That morning in Ha, the men celebrated with these words:

> Occasionally, a beautiful sun rises in the East. Your hit is like the sunrise.

> A double! Such a rare thing, and an example for everyone.

I was studying in the University in Simtokha. There was a girl I admired so much. I tried to get closer to her, but someone else reached her before me. Now that I'm shooting in the archery ground, I must try to reach the target first.

There are two mountains, so close, but they never join at the base because the river cuts through. Your arrow, like the river, cuts straight to the target.

You can find happiness and peace elsewhere, but nothing compares to the happiness and peace of this place.

After lunch, a startling role transformation took place—the ideal portrait of the blending of the conservative and earthy in Bhutan. The female dancers became cheerleaders and teasers. These were beautifully dressed young women, about as sweet and demure as they come. In a flash, they turned into fiendishly clever commentators on the players and their foibles.

The women lined up on the left side of the target, on the "shooting" end of the field. They were almost within touching distance of the shooter. As he drew his bow, the women broke into a frenzied dance and song. It was all impromptu, and the words were chosen to fit the shooter. In something of a miracle, the women knew the words of these custom-designed teases without consulting each other.

And what teases they were.

You won't hit the target, because you look like a black bull, and everyone knows that black bulls can't play archery.

We're looking at your big bump, and we're quite sure there's a lot of semen in there.

You look like a person made out of clay, so you'll never hit the target.

You're a bow-legged man, and bow-legged men never hit the target.

You will not hit the target because you're bald on top, and must be bald down there.

With that beard, you look like a mountain goat. So you can't hit.

You have a big nose, so you're sure to have a big dick. That's convenient, but you won't hit the target.

Where does the earthiness in Bhutanese culture come from? We are not sure we know the whole answer, but it must in part derive from the remarkably sexual nature of Tantric Buddhism. In the sketch "Tantra Demystified," we mentioned that early Tantric Buddhism was anti-establishment to its core, reacting against the institutional forces of 6th-century India. Tantric Buddhism challenged every social convention, encouraging beliefs and behaviors that were outrageous by the standards of prevailing morality. Ultimately, this struggle against authority led to the development of "unexcelled yoga"—a form of meditation by two persons locked in sexual embrace. Tantric Buddhism and unexcelled yoga then migrated to Tibet and shortly thereafter to Bhutan.

We discovered that research in this field is heavy going. We found that most of the writing on sexuality in Tantric Buddhism is either elusive or unintelligible. (More on this later.) However, Richard Robinson and Willard Johnson, in their book *The Buddhist Religion*, have done an outstanding job. Here, we offer excerpts that will go a long way toward illuminating this blend of sex and religion. Where necessary, we have substituted ordinary English, in brackets, for unfamiliar words and phrases.

> The theory underlying the practice of sexual yoga is that impediments to [enlightenment] are actually...knots in the subtle energy channels flowing through the body. On the physical level, these knots are blocks in the energy flow that can be overcome only through the energy aroused by the great passion and bliss "churned" through skillful sexual union....
>
> However, in addition to their physical side, these knots have their emotional and intellectual sides as well. Emotionally, they correspond to inhibitions; intellectually, to dualistic thinking. Thus the texts advocate a psychological program for attacking them. To eradicate inhibitions [they concentrate on] psychological and physical powers repressed by social convention....

To eradicate dualistic thinking, these Tantras advocate a program of mental training to accompany the sexual rite. The [couple] are to stare unblinkingly into each others' eyes, as would a god and goddess, [so that] the sense of "I" and "other" dissolves. The male organ—usually equated with compassion as the "means"—is to be regarded as the vajra, thus erasing the distinction between means and end. The union of the male organ with the female—symbolized as a lotus—is to be viewed as the union of compassion and wisdom; the bliss that arises from the union is to be stripped of all limiting particulars until it becomes Great Bliss, which is then understood as being identical with the emptiness of the Vajra Realm.

One of the most interesting aspects of Unexcelled Yoga...is its use of transgressive sacrality. This principle was not only a sign of the rite's defiant counter cultural status but also a source of its psychological power. It broke taboos, renounced practices that the dominant society regarded as pure and good, and in their place exalted things that society said were impure and bad....In short, the ritual claimed as its own a psychological...territory unclaimed and uncharted by the social sphere. In doing so, it forced ritual participants to confront and overcome the fears that kept uncharted parts of the psyche repressed, with the aim of releasing those forces and harnessing them for power and knowledge....[28]

From your earlier readings in this book, you may be sensing a paradox. You have learned that spiritual leadership in Tantric Buddhism is shared by monks and lamas. And you also know that some monks and lamas are married, while others are celibate. Why would a spiritual leader chose celibacy if enlightenment can only be achieved through sexual meditation?

One solution for celibate Buddhists might be "virtual sex." In Tantric meditation, it is possible to imagine that you are in sexual union with a consort, rather than having a real sexual partner. However, under Tantric doctrine, enlightenment in this lifetime can only be achieved with a real partner. Practicing with an imagined partner is a more problematic path. Why choose virtual sex? Why not the real thing?

Maybe the answer is that Tantrism changed its colors, evolving in the Tibetan Cultural Area from a body of contrarian beliefs to the religion of the establishment. Perhaps an element of prudery and conservatism emerged as Tantric Buddhism became less interested in revolution and more concerned with preservation of social and governmental order. We suspect that two parallel value systems arose, one conservative and the other remarkably liberal.

In our opinion, one can see direct evidence of these contradictory value systems in modern Bhutan. In some ways, the social attitudes of Bhutanese people are strikingly cautious. For example, in the more urban parts of Bhutan, "dating" is almost unknown. Boys and girls in the city are expected to confine their relationships to two modes: casual and unattached, or marriage-bound. The moment a relationship begins to look like the latter, parents get involved. In some settings, the rules applying to boy/girl interactions are draconian. For example, Bhutan's only college (Sherubtse College) has an uncomplicated, intractable rule about dating—it is forbidden.

Yet this book is full of examples of Bhutanese sexual exuberance. These remarkable people simultaneously harbor forbidding and unfettered attitudes toward sex. It is a paradox that delights and confounds a visitor at every turn.

Western attitudes toward Tibet and Tantric Buddhism have bounced back and forth in the most amusing way (which we introduced in the sketch "Sacred Paint"). For example, Victorian explorers and scholars could hardly find the words to express their revulsion over Tibetan Buddhism. In the 1890s, L. Austine Waddell had this to say: "The Lamaist [Tantric Buddhist] cults comprise much deep rooted evil worship, which I describe with some fullness. For Lamaism is only thinly and imperfectly varnished over with Buddhist symbolism, beneath which the sinister growth of poly-demonist superstition darkly appears."[29] The 19th-century explorer Andre Guibaut wrote: "Nowhere but here, in this atmosphere, could the lofty conception of Buddha unite with the dark, primitive rites of ancient Shamanism, to culminate in the monstrosity of Lamaism."[30]

At other times in the 19th and 20th centuries, the Tibetan Cultural Area has been seen as

- the ultimate despotism, ruled by a god-king called the Dalai Lama, or

- a kind of museum in which the people are not so important, but the ancient Sanskrit manuscripts are, or

- a source of cures for almost everything that ails us.

It is that last stereotype that seems to be prevalent now. The Chinese takeover of Tibet was a heart-wrenching event that, for more than 40 years, has generated sorrow and sympathy among Western people. And many of the Tibetan monks who were forced to make a living in foreign countries turned out to be impressive people. In our view, it is only natural that Western people would develop superhuman myths about Tibet, Tantric Buddhism, and the rest of Tibetan culture.

For example, listen to these words from Lama Govinda (an influential writer who, however, was German and a self-appointed lama):

> What is happening in Tibet is symbolic for the fate of humanity. As on a gigantically raised state we witness the struggle between two worlds, which may be interpreted, according to the standpoint of the spectator, either as the struggle between the past and future, between backwardness and progress, belief and science, superstition and knowledge—or as the struggle between spiritual freedom and material power, between the dignity of the human individual and the herd-instinct of the mass, between the faith in the higher destiny of man through inner development and the belief in material prosperity through an ever-increasing production of goods.[31]

More recently, Philip Rawson, author of *Sacred Tibet*, had this to say:

> Its real interest for us is that Tibetan culture offers powerful, untarnished and coherent alternatives to Western egotistical lifestyles, our short attention span, our gradually more pointless pursuit of material satisfactions, and our despair when these, finally, inevitably disappoint us.[32]

In this atmosphere of myth making, one would guess that the modern-day apologists for Tibetan culture would be a little nervous about the earthiness of Tantric Buddhism and about its anti-establishment origins. And so it is. Our bookshelves are full of recent works on Tibetan culture and Tantric Buddhism, written both by Westerners and Himalayans. As a whole, they are sterilized. From our point of view, the smell, feel, and grit of this culture has been banished. In their place are pronouncements that we find pretentious, remote, and painfully politically correct. Not always, but most of the time.

Let us look at the writings of the Dalai Lama himself. We will use his book *The World of Tibetan Buddhism* as an example. We cannot find one word about the shamanic traditions in the Tibetan Cultural Area, which, as you already know from the sketch "The Spirits Within," are deeply interwoven with formal Buddhism and a vibrant part of contemporary religious life. We are unable to get the sense that Tantric Buddhism was revolutionary in its core, intended to turn social conventions inside out.

To the Dalai Lama's credit, he does not duck the question of sexuality altogether. Two pages out of 173 deal with sexual union in unexcelled yoga (which the Dalai Lama calls Highest Yoga). But the words are astonishingly abstract—they make us wonder whether anybody on earth would get the idea.

> As a result of the bodhicitta melting within one's body, the experience of a blissful non-conceptual state arises. If you are able to generate that blissful state into the experience of emptiness, then you have achieved the feat of transforming a delusion into an afflictive emotion, namely, desire. When you are able to utilize that non-conceptual state—that is, the blissful mind—to realize emptiness, the wisdom thus generated becomes exceptionally powerful and serves as the antidote that counteracts all afflictive emotional and cognitive states. Therefore, in one sense, we say that it is delusion itself—in the form of wisdom derived from delusion—that actually destroys the delusions, for it is the blissful experience of emptiness induced by sexual desire that dissolves the force of sexual impulses.[33]

We do not mean to express disrespect for the Dalai Lama and his life work. He is a great man. But we wonder about the writers and editors who serve this warm, spontaneous man. We wonder whether, in their anxiety to support the Dalai Lama's political role, they polish and polish, until the down-to-earth humanity of the author and his culture disappear. We suspect the same thing happens with the majority of those who write about Tibetan Buddhism these days.

In the United States the Tantric tradition is suddenly hot. The action is based more on the residual Hindu Tantric tradition still remaining in India, rather than Tantric Buddhism. But the fundamentals of Hindu and Buddhist Tantra are the same, and the bizarre reinterpretations now emerging in America will probably have important implications for Tantric Buddhism in the future.

In the preceding section, we were a little grumpy about the overly sanitary presentations of Tantra that you typically find in Tantric Buddhist writing. But what is now under way in the U.S. is the opposite. Thanks to the Internet, a bizarre and ultrahyped version of Tantric practice has become a sex-based industry.

Even the *Wall Street Journal* took notice. "Ancient Hindu Sex Practice Gets New Age Makeover," the headline says. They are not kidding.

> In the hands of America's New Age marketers, sex, or "sexual healing" is very much the point, and profit is more often than not the motive. Trading on testimonials from Hollywood celebrities like Woody Harelson and using a vocabulary borrowed from Hinduism and pop psychology, modern Tantra advocates are spinning Tantra into an eccentric market racking up perhaps tens of millions of dollars in annual sales.[34]

We did some research on the Web and found, among others, The Church of Tantra, Tantra.com, The Loving Center, and TantraWorks. Here are some of the great tidbits therein:

> A quote from *Playgirl* Magazine stating that "the ultimate result can be huge, powerful, wildly satisfying orgasms that seem to emanate from the depths of your soul."

An art gallery with downloadable images of couples and groups in every conceivable sexual position.

Tantra vacation seminars in Spa Rio Caliente, Mexico.

Videos of every ilk, including the "Tantric Massage Video" and "Tantric Journey to Female Orgasm, Unveiling the G-spot and Female Ejaculation."

The "Tantric Pleasuring Package," for only $198.00, which includes a rabbit-fur pleasuring mitt and one jar of chocolate bawdy butter.

A crystal vaginal weight-lifting egg ($17.00) promising to increase the strength of your pubococcygeal muscles.

It is hard to know what to say about this. On the one hand, we have a lifelong distaste for practically every trendy, pop-psych thing we have encountered, especially the greedy ones. On the other hand, Tantric practice was rude and crude in its origins, and who are we to say that Tantrism cannot be reinterpreted to facilitate American exploration of forbidden territory?

This is just our personal sense of it, but we wish, for a change, those of us studying Buddhism, and Tantric Buddhism in particular, would be more interested in the middle ground. We wish that apologists for Tibetan Buddhism could be less prudish and abstract. We wish that American popular culture could be less mesmerized by orgasm and more interested in the union of compassion and wisdom. (Good luck!)

In Bhutan, one can find that middle ground. When the moment calls for sober and dignified behavior, the culture delivers. But when it is time to loosen up and to enjoy sexuality as a natural and exuberant part of life, the Bhutanese are masters. Is sex necessary? Yes, indeed.

TARA

Tara is a much-loved female deity who looks upon each living thing as a mother looks upon her child.

FEMALE PERSONS

Our log house on the McKenzie River has a guest bedroom on the ground floor. It is a cozy place, saying "welcome" with gold hues of massive pine logs. A Bhutanese *thangka* hangs on the south wall, and practically every-one who enters the room falls under its spell. At first glance, the painting seems to be just another face-out portrait of a Himalayan deity. But this deity is a female with extraordinary powers of calming and healing. Her name is Green Tara, and she is the most beloved goddess in Bhutan (and indeed in all of the schools of Mahayana Buddhism). Tara is steadily gath-ering admirers in Oregon as well.

When we first encountered the painted images of Tibetan Buddhist deities, it was something of a yawner. We fell into all the standard errors. These paintings seemed rigid, lifeless, and repetitive. As time went by, we realized we were wrong.

Tara is a fine example. Her portrait actually conveys wonderful and intricate messages, but one needs to learn a thing or two about the lan-guage. Start with Tara's right hand. It is curved downward in a position called a *mudra*—a stylized gesture with a specific philosophical mean-ing. In this case, the *mudra* indicates that Tara can provide people with anything they want. Her left hand is also in a *mudra*, generally indicating "refuge." The ring finger and thumb are together, representing the union of wisdom and compassion. (As you know from the sketch "Sacred Paint," the sexual embrace symbolizes the same thing.) The other three fingers are raised, encompassing the three elements of the Buddha's concept of refuge (the Buddha himself, the "law" of Buddhism, and the community of fellow practitioners).

Tara's left leg is in a yoga position, which shows her renunciation of worldly distractions. Her extended right leg proves that she is ready to stand up and help all of us.

One of the intriguing things about Tara is that she comes in different colors. In this case, the color green signals the quality of compassion. (By way of contrast, the white Tara is associated with overcoming life-threatening problems.) Tara sits on a lotus arising from a lake, which reminds us of the idea that Tara herself arose from the compassionate tears of a deity called Avalokiteshvara (a mouthful of a name, but one of the most beloved male deities). Throughout the Himalayas, a prayer to Tara is recited every day by monks and laypeople.

Maybe the best part of the Tara portrait is her overall demeanor. She gazes at each of us with the warmth and clarity of a mother relating to her child. In our experience, it does not matter if the observer is Christian, Jewish, Buddhist, or anything else. We all get the idea.

We imagine that Christians especially relate to Tara. In many ways, Mary is to the Christian religion as Tara is to Buddhism. Both are elemental mother figures who give solace and healing to their admirers. Both are more than human (although Christians are not in the habit of calling Mary a goddess). Both are the object of heartfelt love.

There is another similarity that may not be so commendable. While Tara and Mary both generate more sincere affection than practically any other figures in their respective traditions, the religions themselves have not always been kind to women. The various conservative Christian denominations have tended to keep women out of positions of power and leadership. The same thing is true of Tantric Buddhism. In both cases, if you want the final word on issues of belief and administration, you had better be a man.

Tara is a good introduction to what we might call the "yes—but" status of women in Bhutan. In many ways, Bhutan is literally an island of women's entitlements in Asia. In fact, on a worldwide scale of women's rights, Bhutan stacks up very well. But even in this tolerant society, there are some lingering examples of negative attitudes toward women.

Let us begin with the positive side of the story. In Bhutan, parents are just as happy to have daughters as sons. Bhutan has none of the horrific practices against women seen throughout the world, including female infanticide, bride burning, dowry deaths, and genital mutilation. Women are free to dress and travel as they like (although all Bhutanese are expected to wear national dress in formal settings). While they are sometimes shy in the presence of strangers, Bhutanese women usually have an erect, confident appearance that brings joy to the eyes of anyone who has traveled to countries in which women are treated like possessions.

There is another quality of Bhutanese women that will probably not find its way into scholarly data, but it is striking. Although Bhutanese men love to joke about sex (and so do many women), you do not commonly see sex leading to flamboyant or aggressive behavior. We have not often encountered the endless and tedious preening that we Westerners call "macho." In the chatter among Bhutanese men we have encountered, we generally have not heard men bragging about their penises as instruments of submission or conquest. Sex in Bhutan is, we believe, usually seen as a shared entertainment, not as proof of male superiority.

How do Bhutanese women fare in domestic relations? Bhutan has a law governing marriage, but frequently local practices are just as important. In both the formal and informal frameworks of marriage, women seem to be treated equitably and remarkably better than their counterparts in neighboring Asian countries.

> • Both men and women can initiate a divorce, and divorce is very common.
>
> • If either the husband or wife commits adultery, he or she may be required to pay compensation to the aggrieved spouse (with the amount based on the years of marriage).
>
> • It is legal for a man to have multiple wives and for a woman to have multiple husbands.
>
> • A rapist in Bhutan is required to pay compensation to his female victim and may go to jail.
>
> • Prostitution is legal (although not very visible).
>
> • If a man makes an unmarried woman pregnant, he must pay for her medical treatment and is also required to pay 20 percent of his monthly income for child support.
>
> • Child marriages are prohibited.

Bhutanese women often seem to have the advantage in the realm of property ownership and inheritance. Although these practices vary by region, many women hold title to family property, and the daughters of a family inherit property upon the death of their parents in equal shares. Parents have the final say on the inheritance of property, but they usually follow an equal-share matriarchal pattern.

Interestingly, some Bhutanese women are beginning to think that control of the family property is not such a good deal after all. Ownership might tie them to a difficult life in remote parts of the country. Their sense of stewardship for the land may cut them off from educational opportunities and from better jobs in more urban areas. We have noticed that the Bhutanese, whether they are men are women, can indeed feel trapped by life on the farm, especially if the rest of their family members are chasing what seems to be a more exciting and promising future in the cities.

However, it might be just a matter of time before these perceptions change. As every developing country can attest, life in the cities can be wretched for the new arrivals. Jobs can be scarce, the cost of living is often high, and the support system of an extended family and community is frequently lost. As more Bhutanese people come to understand the limitations of urban life, and as the life of farmers continues to improve, women may universally appreciate the genuinely remarkable system of property ownership in Bhutan. How many of the world's women can say that they own not only the land, but also the houses, grain, cattle, and other material property of a region?

Education of women in Bhutan is a mixed story. The country's school system is coeducational, so females have just as many educational entitlements as males. But fewer girls enroll in school in the first place, and their dropout rate is much higher than boys. Girls who live on farms (which is the great majority of girls in Bhutan) are busy people. Between helping their parents with farm work, caring for siblings, and starting families themselves, farm girls do not have much time for education or entertainment. That could improve over time.

Health care might be a more positive situation. Huge improvements in the health-care system have been made in modern times. All Bhutanese people have equal access to the system, regardless of their gender. The government has made maternal and child health a high national priority. Pregnant women are encouraged to attend prenatal clinics. Women and their children have benefited from a number of government-sponsored nutritional initiatives. Steadily, women's health issues are being reframed to include health-care goals beyond maternal health, including sexually transmitted diseases and mental illness.

Economic development is also a relatively positive realm for women. Bhutan follows the principle of equal pay for equal work in both the private and public sectors. Although women got a slow start in the government, there are now many women in the lower and middle levels of civil service. The government is encouraging women's advancement to higher status. The number of women in the private sector is still small, but as we explain in the sketch "What Lies Ahead," that may be more a reflection of Bhutan's overall difficulty with entrepreneurship than a case of discrimination against women.

After laying out such an impressive list of women's rights in Bhutan, we hesitate to mention the "but" side of the equation. However, just as there may be latent discrimination against women in our own country, so there might be for Bhutanese women.

Notwithstanding Bhutan's outstanding governmental efforts to protect women's rights, and in spite of traditional practices that elevate women, such as property ownership and inheritance, rural women in Bhutan are apparently still perceived as lower in status than men. This point of view appears to be held both by men and women. To be born a woman is sometimes viewed as unlucky and ill-fated.

You can also detect female subjugation in the words used for male and female. Men are often known as *"kep pho,"* which is a relatively honorary term. Women, however, are referred to with the derogatory word *"moringmo."*

Perhaps the most visible form of gender discrimination in Bhutan occurs in the monk body. Although there are Buddhist nuns in Bhutan, they are not numerous and they do not have much power. We are not aware of any movements in Bhutan to shift religious power from men to women. Tibetan Buddhism, in Bhutan and elsewhere, is a male domain.

Earlier in this sketch we mentioned that Bhutanese women often seem visibly more self-confident than women of other developing countries. Were we wrong? Is the reality of female life in Bhutan the same old grim tale of overt and subtle discrimination? Perhaps it is a matter of degree. We have no doubt that Bhutanese women live on a pedestal when compared to the women of many other countries. But, at the heart of the matter, being female, even in progressive Bhutan, might occasionally be a rough road.

Well, no matter what hard-wired gender discrimination we humans seem to possess, at least the Bhutanese are trying mightily to right what is wrong. Perhaps Tara inspires them. When the green lady portrayed in our *thangka* looks at us with those all-knowing eyes, she makes us think of many things: the ultimate importance of a compassionate inner life; the obligation each of us has to set aside prejudice and honor all human beings; especially, the miracles of birth, nurturing, kindness, and other enterprises of female persons.

Lotus

The Lotus symbolizes purity and the opportunity to transcend humble beginnings and develop an elevated spiritual life.

GROSS NATIONAL WHAT?

In 1987, the king of Bhutan said 10 provocative words to a writer from a Western newspaper: "Gross national happiness is more important than gross national product." Ever since, the idea of gross national happiness has been front and center in Bhutanese policy-making.

We admit that we were not sure what to make of "gross national happiness" when we first heard the words. Another sappy platitude by a politician? A heartfelt phrase that was so utopian that it could never be translated to action? A national leader trying to cover up the economic weakness of his country by deflecting attention to a spurious issue? Or a serious national priority that might be unique in the world?

Apparently, our initial puzzlement is shared by other Americans. We have given many presentations about Bhutan to American audiences. Whenever we first mention the idea of GNH, the same thing happens. Some people giggle out loud. Others do a double take, as if they cannot quite believe the words that entered their ears. Looks of disbelief spread across the room. A certain part of the audience is certain that we have cracked a joke and is waiting for the punch line.

But once the ice is broken, Americans are willing to give the idea of GNH a fair hearing. Many of us seem to share the same sense of things—that money, power, position, and the other conventional yardsticks of well-being are on the wrong track. We would be overjoyed with a wiser system of values that nurtured deeper aspirations. American people are, in the end, captivated by the Bhutanese vision of human happiness.

Our reactions to GNH turned positive as we learned more about the author of the concept. We found our admiration for the king of Bhutan, His Majesty Jigme Singye Wangchuck, growing and growing. Here was the unthinkable—an absolute monarch who was visionary, generous, and absolutely honest. We came to realize that the king meant exactly what he said about gross national happiness.

Furthermore, we discovered that government officials and ordinary citizens in Bhutan take GNH seriously indeed. You could make a stack of planning documents two feet high, and every one of them would attempt to test developmental proposals against the happiness of the Bhutanese people. We have never detected the winking of an eye that so often accompanies lofty pronouncements of public policy in other cultures.

One of the best explanations of GNH we have found comes from Bhutan's main environmental planning document, "The Middle Path: National Environment Strategy for Bhutan" (originally written by our friend Karma Ura):

> Historically speaking, economic development has generally been dedicated to improving the quality of life. In Western countries, this has usually meant satisfaction of material wants. According to this conventional definition, a country could only be called "developed" once it reached a certain advanced level of material consumption. On an individual level, this translates into consumerism and materialism.
>
> Compounding the waste and excess inherent in these attributes is their essential progressive and competitive nature. Not only do individuals want to be better off than they were last year, they also want to be better off than neighbors who are seeing their material fortunes improve. Given that the vast majority of these material acquisitions are derived from nature, this geometrically rising pattern eventually exceeds the ability of the surrounding resource base to regenerate itself. Unless consumption patterns are altered or foreign resources can be brought in to fill the gap, the inevitable result is unsustainable development. This dynamic is only accelerated when individually increasing "needs" are compounded by collectively increasing populations.
>
> In Bhutanese culture, however, the original definition of development was based on the acquisition of knowledge. Those who possessed greater knowledge were considered to be more developed. In a similar vein, the process of communal enrichment was based on a dynamic in which those who possessed superior knowledge imparted that

knowledge to others. In the Buddhist religion, this concept of personal development was refined even further to entail overcoming the delusions arising from ignorance, aggression, and the desire for consumption and acquisition.[35]

We have read these paragraphs many times; however, every time we have cause to look at them again, we feel stunned. We cannot keep the "what-ifs" quiet. What if the powerful nations in the world believed that "development" is the acquisition of knowledge? What if knowledgeable people in the rich countries believed that their highest obligation was communal enrichment through the exchange of knowledge? What if personal development were thought, throughout the world, to consist of conquering ignorance, aggression, and the desire for consumption?

The United Nations Development Programme in Bhutan gives us a fascinating opportunity to look at different ideas about development. Bhutan is a client of the UNDP (which is based in a handsome building in the center of the capital city of Thimphu). The UNDP has accomplished some magnificent things for Bhutan (and other developing countries throughout the world), but its concepts of development are different from those of the Bhutanese.

The UNDP uses an index called the "Human Development Index," or more commonly the "HDI."[36] The HDI is a quantified score that is intended to give a quick assessment of a country's accomplishments in human development, compared to about 160 other countries. HDI is calculated by averaging three indicators:

- life expectancy,
- educational attainment, and
- income.

According to this arithmetic, Norway is the place to be (with a number-one ranking). The United States is 6th, behind Australia, Canada, Sweden, and Belgium. The top 48 scores are clumped into the category of "High Human Development." This category includes, by and large, familiar names. There are some surprises, such as Brunei, Uruguay, and Barbados.

What about Bhutan? It does not make the cut for High or Medium Human Development (ranks 49 through 126). Instead, it is number 130, in the Low Human Development category, keeping the company of countries like Haiti and Bangladesh.

What is going on? This is a country in which practically every student educated abroad comes home. It is a place passionately loved by its citizens and governed by men and women whose beliefs about human happiness and development are so eloquent that they give us goose bumps. It is a place whose southern parts are swamped by illegal immigrants from Nepal, even though Nepal and Bhutan receive virtually the same HDI ranking.

There is a hint here that calculating arithmetic averages does not always illuminate the soul of a country. Perhaps the Bhutanese approach to GNH is an important alternative to the HDI.

Although the ideas behind GNH will certainly evolve in the future, the basics seem pretty well in place. According to GNH thinking, the constituents of human happiness cannot be quantified. Some judgment will be required. Four factors are important:[37]

- economic development,
- environmental preservation,
- cultural promotion, and
- good governance.

Notice that the first criterion is the only one overlapping with the UNDP's concept of HDI. (Technically, the HDI can be "extended" to include some data on governance and the environment, but as a practical matter, the HDI normally is based solely on income, life expectancy, and education.) The three remaining criteria in GNH are uniquely Bhutanese. And they are the things for which Bhutan is famous. In fact, you could say that GNH, and the visions planted at its base, stirred us into writing this book. In our opinion, Bhutan's willingness to concentrate on these three goals while keeping materialism within reasonable bounds has caused Bhutan to become a laboratory for human betterment. On a worldwide scale, this country may be one of a kind.

That said, we must also be honest about the challenges. It is not always easy to convert the abstractions of GNH into down-to-earth decision making. The Bhutanese face some of the same trade-offs and "no free lunch" puzzles that we Westerners do. Take hydropower as an example.

Hydropower would, at face value, seem to fit perfectly into the philosophy of GNH. Hydroelectric projects in Bhutan are almost all "run of the river," taking advantage of Bhutan's steep terrain. These projects do not need dams or reservoirs. Instead, water is dropped through pipes for 2,000 feet or more, producing the energy to turn hydroelectric turbines. Thus hydropower seems to be one of the few forms of development in Bhutan that could improve the life of the people without damaging the environment.

But it is not so simple. Hydropower cannot be sustained unless the watershed in the area is rigorously protected. That means that towns cannot grow, farmers' fields cannot be expanded, and road construction must be limited. All of these imperatives can cause human suffering in a country whose population is growing and whose new lives must be fed, clothed, and housed.

Development of the private sector is another example. In the old days, Bhutan was a country of farmers, monks, and rulers. Some people traded and ran tiny shops, but their numbers were few. Everyone had a job to do.

At the beginning of the 20th century, the current dynasty of kings took over. Increasingly, the Bhutanese people felt comfortable delegating everything complex or developmental to the government. That worked for a while, as the government vigorously attacked problems in health care, education, transportation, environmental preservation, and protection of the culture. And everyone still had a job to do.

But things are different in modern Bhutan. The government realizes that it has just about reached the limit of its ability to tackle all the complex problems single-handedly. It simply does not have enough money to take the country's systems of health care, transportation, and education to the next level. The government understands that many of the crucial tasks in Bhutan must now be undertaken by the private sector.

The problem is that the private sector hardly exists. The country's shopkeepers and traders do not have the vision, capital, or management skills for private-sector solutions to large-scale social initiatives. The tiny number of businesspeople in Bhutan who have tried to establish more modern business enterprises have sometimes experienced lukewarm support or hostility from the government. While the country is now fortunate to have a substantial number of young people with excellent educations, they are not able to find older businesspeople to serve as mentors or employers. Suddenly, some of the best and brightest workers in the country do not have meaningful jobs to do.

Thus there are now compelling reasons to promote capitalism and entrepreneurship in Bhutan. But herein lie some of the deepest puzzles a nation can face. Would a more vigorous and capitalistic private sector be kind to the environment? Would it tend to protect the culture? Would the pressure to earn a buck start to erode the honesty and competence of the government?

And so it goes—one set of wrenching trade-offs after another. How is poverty actually weighed against spiritual growth? Does a genuine commitment to traditional Buddhist values condemn a culture to high rates of infant mortality, unsafe water, and respiratory diseases? Will the noble vision of gross national happiness ultimately deny the people of Bhutan the health and comfort that much of the world takes for granted?

It is a struggle, but maybe that is the point. It is not easy for the Bhutanese to find the middle path, but they still endeavor mightily to uncover it. Over and over, they raise the prickly questions, tussle with the trade-offs, try to cup their hands around the flame of their culture. The rest of us routinely sacrifice elements of environment, culture, and governance in a way that would break the hearts of our friends in Bhutan.

We close this sketch with the words of Lyonpo Jigme Thinley, delivered to a United Nations planning meeting. If we had an extra million dollars or so, we would rent a Boeing 737 and fly Lyonpo Jigme Thinley to the capitals of the world, spreading a point of view we sorely need to hear.

> There is a paradox here: excessive preoccupation with our selves does not lead to real knowledge of ourselves. Happiness depends, instead, on gaining freedom from this particular kind of self concern....In our opinion, minimizing of self concern is also an important step in the process of constructing a happier web of human relationships, and of transforming man into a less intrusive and destructive force in our natural and human environments. Man

is just a sentient being, among other forms of existence. The assumption that man is on top of the chain of beings is misplaced, considering the mysterious web of inter-dependent relationships that is now being confirmed through scientific studies. Reality is not hierarchical but a whole, circular, enclosed system. Sustainable development is, therefore, in the interest of every being, every day, not just in the interest of future generations alone. A strong ethic of conservation, underpinned by the beliefs just described, influence Bhutanese environmental policies.[38]

What Lies Ahead?

Every time we visit Bhutan, we are left with the same feeling—this place must be honored. Not just for the Bhutanese people, but for the rest of us. The millions of us who are searching for a more balanced inner life and who hunger for a vibrant connection with the natural world need Bhutan to prosper. There may be no place on earth that can better teach us wiser ways to live.

Bhutan's prosperity may be a tall order. It is a speck between two enormous countries, China and India, that have a history of absorbing their neighbors. It is practically unknown to the outside world. Its culture—Tantric Buddhism—has been crushed in Asia and is morphing in the West. Its core values of spiritual growth and economic restraint are probably the object of scorn or indifference to the great majority of surrounding populations. It does not have the financial reserves, military might, or strategic importance to protect itself.

Every year, Bhutan engages in "border discussions" with China. It may seem startling, but China claims Bhutanese territory (all the way to the middle of the Paro Valley). Bhutan has been fearful of China ever since China's takeover of Tibet. These annual discussions must keep the Bhutanese awake at night.

India poses a different, but comparably weighty, threat to Bhutan's future. On the one hand, Bhutan depends on India for many things, including trained professionals, developmental capital, military assistance, food, manufactured goods, access to international seaports and airports, and a marketplace for Bhutan's hydroelectric power. On the other, there is a constant danger that Indian influences may some day swamp Bhutan's culture. That is what happened to Bhutan's neighboring Buddhist kingdom of Sikkim. As a consequence, Sikkim lost many of its cultural roots, and all of its independence, in becoming a part of India.

In this sketch, we ask, What will be crucial to Bhutan's survival? Some of the issues we raise are well known to the Bhutanese and are thoroughly documented in their national planning documents. Others have come to us as a result of our service in that country. We hope the Bhutanese people reading this text will not mind if we pass along some insights that we Westerners are learning the hard way.

First, there is one matter that we will mention in passing. Bhutan suffers from a torment that is constantly in the minds of the people and, as we understand it, is a grave concern to the king and the government. In a nutshell, the southern border of Bhutan tends to be an unstable and unhappy place. The southern regions are often used as sanctuaries by groups who are in armed rebellion against India, seeking autonomy. Furthermore, many Nepali-speaking residents of Bhutan (both citizens and squatters) are unhappy with the government, feeling that they are the victims of discriminatory policies.

We elected not to plunge into the southern border problem in this book. To do it justice, we would need to explore local politics at a level of detail that would probably put most of our readers asleep. Further, the details of this issue change constantly. Many of the things we could say here about the southern problem would be out-of-date by the time this book is published.

This sketch attempts to look at the more systemic questions relating to Bhutan's survival. What fundamental things must happen to give this little country staying power? Given the reality that Bhutan will never have meaningful military power in comparison to its neighbors, how will it accumulate the other assets of survival, such as financial independence, international visibility, and cultural cohesion?

In our opinion, one of the most important issues of all, as in much of the world, is growth in population. Paradoxically, Bhutan, at superficial levels, seems underpopulated. Huge parts of the country have no people at all. There is a chronic scarcity of labor, and many "guest workers" are brought to Bhutan to build roads and construct buildings. The Bhutanese like to say that their country is the least populated in Asia.

Appearances are misleading. Much of the vacant land in Bhutan is too high or too steep to support people. A high percentage has been set aside in Bhutan's commendable effort to preserve its biodiversity in national parks. In reality, the amount of excellent arable land in Bhutan is almost vanishingly small, and virtually all of it has been farmed for centuries.

A few years ago, Bhutan's prognosis for population growth seemed grim. Although the government's planning documents said all the right things—about the need to improve reproductive health, employment opportunities for women, and education for those living in rural areas—the country's rate of population growth jumped to 3.1 percent per year (very high by international standards). And a large number of young women were poised to enter their reproductive years.

A wonderfully refreshing change may be taking place. The government declared that it was on a "war footing" with the population problem, and its efforts to reduce the rate of increase have actually seemed to work. The rate is now down to 2.5 percent per year, and some respected authorities think that it may drop to the replacement rate by the year 2010. If that happens, then Bhutan will have pulled off a miracle, overcoming one of the most intractable problems in the world of developing nations.

Our second survival issue is a sleeper. It has to do with learning. Even if Bhutan resolves all of its other survival problems, the country's future will depend on the adaptability and brain power of its people. This little place will persist by living by its wits.

We have no hesitations about the essential intellectual capability of the Bhutanese people. They are both subtle and deep thinkers. Any population in which the typical person speaks three to five languages and can deal with the intricacies of Tantric Buddhism has what it takes. But there are some things about education in modern Bhutan that worry us. We are not entirely sure Bhutanese people are getting the reasoning tools they need for the 21st century.

The learning issue was first dramatized for us during a hike with our friend Rinchen Yoezer in the Oregon Cascades. At the time, Rinchen was a graduate student at the University of Oregon. He was an excellent student and fully deserved the comprehensive scholarship he had received for his graduate studies.

As we walked through the Douglas fir forests on the way to Castle Rock, we talked about the hurdles Rinchen needed to overcome before he was admitted to the graduate school. One of the big steps was the GRE (graduate record exam). We made the usual grumbles about what a challenging test it is, and then Rinchen stunned us. "The GRE was the first reasoning test I had taken in my life," he said.

In the minds of two Americans, it was incomprehensible that a serious student, well into his twenties, could say this. First, we were flabbergasted that he could pass the GRE. Second, we were disheartened that a student could dwell at least 16 years in the educational system of Bhutan without being asked to reason out an answer on a test.

Since then, we have encountered more evidence about the "Indian model" of education prevailing in Bhutan. The reports are always the same. This approach to learning is based on rote memorization. Deductive skills are not encouraged or expected. Of course, one could argue that rote learning is the norm throughout much of Asia and that many Asian countries have prospered. That argument is correct on its face, but, in our opinion, might miss the point. We suspect that prosperity in Asia might be based on cultural qualities, such as work ethics and loyalty. Asian success might have been achieved in spite of, and not because of, the rote memory philosophy of education.

In any event, we believe that the rote model of education is dangerous for Bhutan. Bhutan cannot tolerate inflexible and dogmatic forms of learning. The nation will survive only because Bhutanese people are able to reason through new solutions to unexpected problems, not because they have committed facts to memory.

There is another aspect of learning in Bhutan that makes us nervous. While many people in urban areas have magnificent skills in spoken languages, including English, Dzongkha, Nepali, Hindi, and regional dialects, we do not know many Bhutanese who love to read. (One notable exception is a friend who owns so many books that their combined weight cracked the floor of his house.) Thimphu, the capital city, has about one and a half bookstores, and they do not do a land office business. It has one tiny community library, which took us six years to find. The very handsome National Library in Thimphu seems to be populated primarily by a small number of scholars, not by citizens.

We believe that self-confidence and enthusiasm for reading, especially in English, will be fundamental to Bhutan's future. There is no other way the people will acquire enough knowledge of the outside world and evolving technologies to prosper in the coming century. The government will not be able to spoon-feed the information the people need. Bhutan's citizens will have to develop it themselves, and therefore will need to become skillful, fast, and motivated readers.

To be fair, Bhutan's educational system and literacy rates have moved miraculous distances from the time, only four or five decades ago, when almost the only educational opportunity in the country was religious training in monasteries. But Bhutan needs to survive in a rough world in which many of its Asian competitors have huge head starts. To play this game, the Bhutanese people must have the knack of self-improvement; reading skills will be at the heart of the matter.

Our third survival issue relates to the tiny group of people the Bhutanese call the "private sector." The Bhutanese recognize that the government has just about reached its limits as an employer of young people. They know that jobs for future generations (and, indeed, for a sizable part of the current generation) must come from men and women who have the courage, knowledge, and money to operate businesses. Consequently, there are constant calls for more development of the private sector.

The problem is that little happens. Apart from stirring up the travel business, most efforts to get the private sector rolling seem to be much talk and little do. Of course, Bhutan is hardly alone here; the issue of the private sector is encountered in many developing countries.

What is different about Bhutan is that there may be a moral undertone to the private sector dilemma. As you know from the sketch "Gross National Happiness," the Bhutanese people believe that spiritual growth is more important than material wealth. There are countless examples, at both the national and personal level, of Bhutanese who turn their backs on economic opportunities, to have a better chance of achieving inner happiness. In our opinion, this rare and commendable view of life sometimes backfires. In particular, we think it tends to create a jaundiced view of business ventures and of the people who pursue them. On many occasions, we have noticed subtle but powerful signals in Bhutan that doing business is not quite honorable.

Another force is at work. Bhutan is a vertical place. Leadership and authority are held in high esteem, whether they are encountered in schools, government, or monasteries. We believe that the Bhutanese peoples' natural respect for authority is interfering with the effort to expand the private sector. For example, even though government jobs do not pay very much, and even though they are often tangled up in a slow-moving, frustrating bureaucracy, they are still the hot jobs for Bhutanese young people. Landing a job in the private sector was traditionally viewed as an embarrassment, a form of failure.

Yet another feature of Bhutanese culture slows down the emergence of the private sector. Fifty years ago, practically everyone in this country was a farmer, living in a noncash economy. Today, most people still are. Therefore, very few Bhutanese people really have business skills bred in the bone. Almost no one has deep experience with tools we consider fundamental, including information systems, generally accepted accounting principles, security instruments, and commercial legal remedies. In fact, many Bhutanese, having been raised in a world of barter transactions, do not understand money very well. Often they do not understand that debts must be repaid on time and in full. And because the Bhutanese attitude toward the passage of time is so easygoing, few of them grasp that time is money.

A high percentage of upper-level students in Bhutan are studying business and commerce. But sometimes we wonder whether anything useful sinks in. We suspect that what these young people really need is not teachers talking about business issues in which the teachers themselves have no experience, but impressive role models in the community

For all these reasons, the problem of the private sector is a tough one. Here is a realm where Western skills may be useful. In general, we feel that the Bhutanese have more to teach us than we have to teach them. But with respect to the private sector, Western people have much to give. If we were advisers to the king, we would encourage him and the government to do whatever it takes to attract upstanding, experienced, and honest Western businesspeople to get involved with Bhutanese commerce and education, and to teach both by book learning and by example.

In our judgment, the Bhutanese underestimate the help they could receive from Western people—for no money, and just by asking. We cannot count the number of sophisticated, good-hearted Westerners who have asked us how they might be able to do public service in Bhutan. These people are not looking for IOUs or hooks; they just want to do their small part in preserving one of the world's extraordinary cultures. But we have discovered that people in Bhutan often do not know what to make of the philanthropic spirit. Philanthropy is not well established in Bhutan. Thus the Bhutanese cannot quite believe that Westerners are willing to help their country with no strings attached.

The irony is that "giving back to the community" is almost the defining characteristic of many Westerners in their fifties and sixties. The Western world is full of magnificent men and women with every business skill in the book who would be only too happy to make their personal contributions to Bhutan. It is just a question of getting them organized.

Another survival issue looks, at first blush, like a subset of the private sector question, but it is important on its own merits. It is the question of tourism. Up to this point, the Bhutanese have handled tourism very well. They have attracted high-end travelers who have enough money to contribute to the economy and are generally respectful of the environment and culture. The tourist infrastructure, such as buses, hotels, and places to eat, is reasonably well matched to the demand.

But the Bhutanese tend to look at tourism as just another business. It appears in lists that also include hydropower, cement, and farm products. We believe that tourism has two roles in Bhutan—as a business, which is well understood, and as an instrument of foreign policy, which is not.

To survive, Bhutan needs exposure to the outside world. Since it has no strategic importance to any countries other than India and China, who would really care if it were absorbed by one of its neighbors? But Bhutan cannot afford the usual mechanisms for international exposure. It has embassies in just a few countries and could not pay the cost of more. Although Bhutan is a member of the United Nations, it does not otherwise have access to the inner chambers of international power.

Here may be the real importance of tourism. Most people who travel in Bhutan are left with positive feelings, especially if they have traveled to other Himalayan destinations, such as Tibet and Nepal, during the same trip. Quite a few travelers to Bhutan, including us, fall in love with the place. In our opinion, tourism in Bhutan should not be managed just as a business. It should be shaped and operated as the most powerful, and least expensive, form of international bridge building this country will ever have.

Our final survival issue feels like jousting windmills. It is the "boob tube," otherwise known as television. For a long time, television was illegal in Bhutan. The ban was lifted in 1999, at the same time the 25th anniversary of the king was being celebrated. The Internet was introduced to the country concurrently.

We believe that the arrival of the Internet was clearly in the best interests of the country. It is already serving as a vital lifeline of knowledge for people in the urban areas of Bhutan. And email has revolutionized international communications. For the first time in its history, Bhutan has a cheap and reliable way to stay in touch with the outside world.

But we think television is another story. Bhutan is now flooded with satellite channels, most of which show various cultures around the world at their most banal and violent. In Thimphu, television sets drone on and on in virtually every place that people gather. Maybe it is just our problem, but we believe it is astonishing that the most popular television programming seems to be professional wrestling from America. Crowds of Bhutanese gather around their televisions, watching some of the strangest people America has ever produced pummeling each other.

Earlier in this sketch, we said that Bhutan's survival assets might be financial independence, international visibility, and cultural cohesion. Television attacks that third factor. Sneaking into a culture in sheep's clothing, it threatens to drain the vitality from traditional culture, turning the values of a country into cartoons.

In an effort to confront the adverse consequences of television, the government produces some local programming aimed at supporting Bhutanese culture. But it is just a few hours a day and operates on a shoestring. It does not stand a chance against Indian soap operas, Western violence, and the rest of the nasty and inane stuff in which television often seems to specialize. Most Bhutanese we know look at television as entertaining and harmless. And it is true that there is practically nothing else to do at night in Bhutan—television is occupying a vacuum that has been there for a long time. However, in our view, the Bhutanese do not understand the insidious and destructive consequences of television.

One of the most wonderful things about Bhutan is the lovely, time-consuming, and sensitive pace of most public events. Festival dances, for example, take hours to perform, and archery tournaments go on all day. We think that television could damage all of that, at least in the urban areas. Within five years or less, we fear that if an event is not frenetic (and simplistic), it might fail.

We are also concerned that television might obscure the moral issues of violence. While videos (which have been available in Bhutan for quite some time) have already gone down that path, television seems to us the ultimate brainwasher. We believe that the gentle, tolerant, and courtly manners of the Bhutanese are at risk. Will those beautiful values survive, when night after night the people soak in the pushy, rude, and violent behaviors of so many characters on television?

Television could have another adverse consequence. It might depress the people's motivation to read. As we have already mentioned, reading might already be a problem in Bhutan. Based on our observations in our own country, we believe that television could multiply that problem several times over.

Television will work, 24 hours a day, to change other Bhutanese values in a thousand little ways. We are reminded of the impact of television on Fiji, as reported by the columnist Ellen Goodman.[39] Not long ago, Fiji, like Bhutan, had no television. Then it arrived. Unlike Bhutan, there was only one channel.

Up to that point, the Fijians had venerated stout people. In their value system, large men and women were robust, handsome creatures. But television is preoccupied with thin people. Within 38 months, the number of young people suffering eating disorders doubled, and the number of girls who vomited for weight control increased 500 percent. Seventy-four percent of teenagers in Fiji reported that they felt too big or fat. In three years, people who had been honored in Fijian society were seen as repulsive.

What to do? The answer is not to reimpose the ban on television. That kind of heavy-handed social control is incompatible with the progressive nature of Bhutan's government. We suppose that the only answer is to pour resources into the production of Bhutanese programming, preserving and deepening the traditional culture. We feel that parent education is also crucial. Parents need to be taught that leaving their children in front of the television for hours at a time is a plug-in drug. The consequences can be depressing.

What does lie ahead? Will Bhutan survive? Will it continue to be a laboratory for the exploration of values and lifestyles, unique in the world?

We suppose that the answer is a conditional yes. Yes, if the Bhutanese people have the grit and discipline to confront some of the issues in this sketch. Yes, if enough of the world's people are serious about preserving a place that teaches us how to set aside our hunger for things, improve our minds, honor the earth, and achieve a measure of inner peace.

Bhutan's king is at the center of our hopeful feelings for the future. We have never encountered a political figure quite like him. The adjectives might sound unreal, but they have been earned—wise, generous, steady, unpretentious, and utterly dedicated to the people of Bhutan. Jigme Singye Wangchuck is a universal role model for leadership.

We wrote this book as our small contribution to the future of Bhutan. Other people, both Bhutanese and visitors, are making their own investments in the country, some far more important than ours. We are all stirred into action by the same thing. This country really is different. It rekindles dreams we once had of working for greater generosity and sensitivity in our society. It encourages us to reach for higher planes, even if we had felt our optimism about the human condition ebbing.

May the future be kind to Bhutan.

NOTES

1. Karma Ura, *The Hero with a Thousand Eyes: A Historical Novel* (Thimphu, Bhutan, 1995), 359.

2. Christian Schicklgruber, "Gods and Sacred Mountains," in *Bhutan: Mountain Fortress of the Gods,* ed. Christian Schicklgruber and Françoise Pommaret (New Delhi, Bookwise [India] Pvt Ltd, 1997), 166.

3. *Ibid.,*159.

4 Geoffrey Samuel, *Civilized Shamans: Buddhism in Tibetan Societies* (Washington and London, Smithsonian Institution Press, 1993), 179

5 *Ibid.,* 162-163.

6. *Ibid.,* 297.

7. Matthieu Ricard, *Journey to Enlightenment: The Life and World of Khyentse Rinpoche, Spiritual Teacher from Tibet* (Aperture, undated), 45.

8. *Ibid.,* 52.

9. *Ibid.,* 72.

10. *Ibid.,* 108.

11. Samuel, *Civilized Shamans,* 285.

12. Mircea Eliade, ed., *The Encyclopedia of Religion* (New York, Simon & Schuster Macmillan, 1995), 14:273.

13. Donald S. Lopez, Jr., *Prisoners of Shangri-La: Tibetan Buddhism and the West* (Chicago and London, The University of Chicago Press, 1998), 145.

14. *Ibid.,* 145.

15. Marylin M. Rhie and Robert A. F. Thurman, *Wisdom and Compassion: The Sacred Art of Tibet* (New York, Tibet House New York, 1991), 17-18.

16. Ian A. Baker, *The Tibetan Art of Healing* (New Delhi, Timeless Books, 1997), 7.

17. *Ibid.,* 58.

18. *Eighth Five Year Plan* (Thimphu, Bhutan, Ministry of Planning, Royal Government of Bhutan, 1996), chapter 28.

19. *The Paro Resolution on Environment and Development.*

20. *The Middle Path: National Environment Strategy for Bhutan* (Thimphu, Bhutan, National Environment Commission, Royal Government of Bhutan, 1997), 37.

21. Keith Dowman, trans., *The Divine Madman: The Sublime Life and Songs of Drukpa Kunley* (Middletown, California, The Dawn Horse Press, 1998), xxxiv-xxxv

22. *Ibid.,* 47.

23. *Ibid.,* 24-26.

24. *Ibid.,* 64.

25. *Ibid.,* 72-73.

26. *Ibid.,* 76-77.

27 *Ibid.,* 96-98.

28. Richard H. Robinson and Willard L. Johnson, *The Buddhist Religion: A Historical Introduction* (London and other cities, Wadsworth Publishing Company, 1997), 127-129.

29 Lopez, *Prisoners of Shangri-La,* 161.

30 *Ibid.,* 4.

31 *Ibid.,* 7.

32 Philip Rawson, *Sacred Tibet* (London, Thames and Hudson Ltd, 1991), 5.

33. The Dalai Lama, *The World of Tibetan Buddhism* (Boston, Wisdom Publications, 1995), 97.

34. Assra Q. Nomani, "Tantra May be Old, But It has Generated a Hot Modern Market," *The Wall Street Journal,* December 7, 1998.

35. *The Middle Path,* 3.

36. See the section "Analytical Tools for Human Development" within the UNDP web site. At the time this book was written, the URL was http://www.undp.org/hdro/anatools.htm.

37. *Gross National Happiness* (Thimphu, Bhutan, Centre for Bhutan Studies, 1999), 9

38. *Ibid.,* 18-19.

39. Ellen Goodman, "The Culture of Thin Bites Fiji Teens," *The Boston Globe,* May 27, 1999.

GLOSSARY

Atsara—a clown at religious festivals. Atsara often carries a large wooden penis and specializes in ribald humor.

Bon—commonly used to refer to the religion practiced in the Himalayas before the arrival of Buddhism. However, Bonpo is also a modern religion, still practiced in Bhutan, Tibet, and neighboring areas.

Bumthang—a general name given to a region of four valleys in Central Bhutan.

chorten—Buddhist monuments found by the thousands in Bhutan. *Chortens* tend to be small structures in the shape of a flat-sided pillar, but there are a few large ones, with different geometries. The Sanskrit term is *stupa*.

dorje (also *vajra*)—an object frequently cast in metal and often appearing in the hands of deities. It has many meanings, but perhaps the most common one is "thunderbolt." The Dorje represents the male principle of compassion.

druk—the dragon. An important symbol in Bhutan, because Bhutan itself is known as the "Dragon Kingdom," or *"Druk Yul."*

Drukpa Kunley—a 16th-century "crazy saint" who traveled extensively in Tibet and Bhutan.

dzong—large buildings in Bhutan that originally served as combined fortresses and monasteries. In modern times, they often house government offices and various Buddhist facilities.

Dzongkha—the national language of Bhutan, based on a dialect from Western Bhutan.

gelong—an ordained, celibate monk who wears a monk's robe and generally lives in a *gompa* or *dzong*.

gho—the national dress for men.

gomchen—religious leaders who straddle the line between the monastic community and ordinary village life. Many are members of the Nyingma order.

gompa—a Buddhist monastery.

Guru Rinpoche—the Buddhist saint who brought Buddhism to Bhutan in the 8th century.

Je Khenpo—the Chief Abbot of Bhutan.

Jichu Drake—a mountain peak in Western Bhutan, and also the name of the local deity who lives there.

Jigme Singye Wangchuck—the fourth and current king of Bhutan.

Kagyu—an order of Buddhism and the state religion of Bhutan. Technically, the branch in Bhutan is known as Drukpa Kagyupa.

karma—the results of the actions of one's past life on one's current life.

kira—the national dress for women.

lama—a Buddhist master. May be celibate or married. May live in a religious setting, or at home.

Lopen—title given to learned people, especially monks

lu—a female water deity, half human and half reptile.

lhakhang—a Buddhist temple, generally larger than a *chorten* and often smaller that a *gompa*.

mani **wall**—a stone wall with carved Buddhist prayers.

mantra—Sanskrit syllables recited in a chant, directed at a particular meditational deity.

mudra—stylized hand gestures with specific religious meanings. Found in almost all the wall paintings of deities.

Nyingma—a Buddhist order. Although a different order—the Kagyu—is the state religion of Bhutan, the Nyingma school is important. The two schools overlap considerably, but the Nyingma order tends to be less formal.

Padmasambhava—the Sanskrit name for Guru Rinpoche. Also viewed as one of Guru Rinpoche's eight "manisfestations."

Paro—an important city in Western Bhutan. Bhutan's only airport is located in the Paro Valley.

Pema Lingpa—an important 16th century *terton* (finder of treasures) and an ancestor of many prominent people in modern Bhutan.

prayer flags—long strips of cloth printed with prayers that are "said" whenever the wind blows

prayer wheel—a cylindrical wheel inscribed with and containing prayers.

Rinpoche—generally refers to reincarnates of great lamas. The reincarnates may themselves be accomplished people, or may be ordinary citizens.

Shabdrung—a 17th century leader who unified Bhutan for the first time.

tantra—texts that contain the beliefs and rituals of Tantric Buddhism.

Tantric Buddhism—the Buddhism of Bhutan and the Tibetan Cultural Area. Synonymous with Tibetan Buddhism and Vajrayana.

terma—hidden religious artifacts, frequently texts.

terton—a person who finds *terma*.

thangka—a scroll work of art, frequently painted, sometimes embroidered.

Thimphu—the capital city of Bhutan, located in the western part of the country.

Tibetan Cultural Area—an amorphous term applying to the vast region in which Tibetan culture has been influential, including Bhutan.

tulku—a person who is the reincarnation of a past religious master.

Ugyen Wangchuck—the first king of Bhutan, who came to power in 1907.

yathra—colorful handwoven woolen cloth, frequently with geometric designs, woven in the Bumthang region.

Recommended Reading

Just a few books have concentrated on Bhutan. We feel these are the best for the non-academic reader. A number of them may be out of print and/or difficult to locate.

Bhutan, by Françoise Pommaret. (Contemporary Books; ISBN: 0844299669; 3rd edition, 1999) The best of several travel guides by a true expert on Bhutan.

Bhutan: Mountain Fortress of the Gods, edited by Christian Schicklgruber and Françoise Pommaret. (Serindia Publ; ISBN: 0906026490; 2000) Handsome format, variable quality in the articles.

Bhutan: Kingdom of the Dragon, by Robert Dompnier. (Shambhala Publ; ASIN: 1570625107; 1999) A coffee-table book with fine photography.

Birds of Bhutan, by Carol Inskipp, Tim Inskipp, and Richard Grimmett. (A&C Black; ISBN: 0713651636; 1999) Bird watching in Bhutan can be great fun. This is a superior guide.

From the Land of the Thunder Dragon: Textile Arts of Bhutan, edited by Diana K. Myers and Susan S. Bean. (Weatherhill; ISBN: 0906026334; 1995) Extremely skillful and interesting treatment of textiles and their important role in Bhutanese culture.

Lonely Planet Bhutan, by Stan Armington. (Lonely Planet; ISBN: 1864501456; 2nd edition; 2002) Another excellent travel guide.

Of Rainbows and Clouds: The Life of Yab Ugyen Dorji as Told to His Daughter, by Ashi Dorji Wangmo Wangchuck. (Serindia Publ; ISBN: 0906026490; 2000) An appealing look at traditional Bhutan written by one of Bhutan's queens.

So Close to Heaven: The Vanishing Buddhist Kingdoms of the Himalayas, by Barbara Crossette. (Knopf; ASIN: 067941827X; 1995) A competent survey of Tantric Buddhist enclaves including Bhutan.

The Hero with a Thousand Eyes, by Karma Ura. (Karma Ura; ISBN: 81-7525-001-1; 1995) A gripping look at Bhutan's emergence from a feudal society in the form of a novel based on the life of Shingkhar Lam.

The Jesuit and the Dragon, by Howard Solverson. (Robert Davies Publ; ISBN: 1895854377; 1996) An intriguing story of Father William Mackey's experiences in Bhutan beginning in the 1960s.

The Raven Crown: The Origins of Buddhist Monarchy in Bhutan, by Michael Aris. (Weatherhill; ISBN: 0906026326; 1995) May be too detailed for the average reader, but excellent writing by a respected scholar.

In contrast, an enormous number of books have been published on Tantric Buddhism and Tibet. For the issues discussed by *The Blessings of Bhutan*, these have proved to be especially useful.

Buddhism without Beliefs, by Stephen Batchelor. (Riverhead Books, ISBN: 1-57322-058-2; 1997) A confession—this book does not actually focus on Tibet. However, it is an uplifting reminder that Western people can unearth the insights of Buddhism.

Civilized Shamans: Buddhism in Tibetan Societies, by Geoffrey Samuel. (Smithsonian Institution Press, ISBN: 1-56098-231-4; 1993) An astonishingly intelligent, clear-headed view of Tibetan culture.

Journey to Enlightenment: The Life and World of Khyentse Rinpoche, Spiritual Teacher from Tibet, by Matthieu Ricard. (Aperture; ISBN; 0-89381-679-5, undated) A treasure at all levels.

Prisoners of Shangri-La; Tibetan Buddhism and the West, by Donald S. Lopez, Jr. (University of Chicago Press, ISBN: 0-226-49310-5, 1998) Professor Lopez deflates some of the mythology about Tibetan culture.

The Divine Madman: The Sublime Life and Songs of Drukpa Kunley, translated by Keith Dowman. (The Dawn Horse Press; ISBN 0-913922-75-7; 2nd ed; 1998) The life and teachings of a truly engaging character.

The World of Tibetan Buddhism, by the Dalai Lama. (Wisdom Publ; ISBN: 0-86717-097-5; 1995) In the end, all thinking about Tantric Buddhism needs to be tested against the teachings of the Dalai Lama. Among his many books, this one will serve that purpose well.

Wisdom and Compassion: The Sacred Art of Tibet, by Marylin M. Rhie and Robert A. F. Thurman. (Harry N. Abrams; ISBN: 0-8109-3985-1; 1996) An indispensable compendium of Tibetan art.

INDEX